HARD-CORE HOCKEY

Essential Skills, Strategies, and Systems from the Sport's Top Coaches

. . .

RAND PECKNOLD, HEAD COACH,
QUINNIPIAC UNIVERSITY, WITH AARON FOESTE
PHOTOGRAPHS BY BRUCE CURTIS

New York   Chicago   San Francisco   Lisbon   London   Madrid   Mexico City
Milan   New Delhi   San Juan   Seoul   Singapore   Sydney   Toronto

The **McGraw·Hill** Companies

Library of Congress Cataloging-in-Publication Data

Pecknold, Rand.
　　　Hard-core hockey : skills, strategies, and systems from the sport's top college coaches
　/ Rand Pecknold ; with Aaron Foeste. — 1st ed.
　　　　　p.　　cm.
　　　ISBN: 978-0-07-148045-1 (alk. paper)
　　　　1. Hockey—Training.　　I. Foeste, Aaron.　　II. Title.

　GV848.3.P43　　2008
　796.962—dc22　　　　　　　　　　　　　　　　　　2008023758

1 2 3 4 5 6 7 8 9 10 11 12 13 14 15 16 17 18 19 20 21 22 23　DOC/DOC　0 9

ISBN　978-0-07-148045-1
MHID　　0-07-148045-5

Photographs by Bruce Curtis, except as otherwise noted

McGraw-Hill books are available at special quantity discounts to use as premiums and sales promotions or for use in corporate training programs. To contact a representative, please visit the Contact Us pages at www.mhprofessional.com.

This book is printed on acid-free paper.

Thank you to my wife, Nikki, for her love and support.
To my father, Wayne, for teaching me the game.
And to my mother, Jeannie, for taking me to all those
6:00 A.M. hockey practices.

Contents

Acknowledgments

There are a number of individuals who, through their expertise, helped me complete this project.

Thank you to Mike Kobylanski, sports information director at Quinnipiac University until 2007 and now the associate athletic director for sports information at Southern Connecticut State University, who was instrumental in helping me finish this book. Thank you also to Ken Sweeten, the current sports information director at Quinnipiac University, who also played a part in writing this book and helping with the illustrations.

And thank you to Ben Syer, Scott Robson, and Duncan Fletcher, who played a major role in designing the practice drills in Chapter 7.

Key to Diagrams

F = Forward
D = Defenseman
RD = Right defenseman
LD = Left defenseman
SD = Strong-side defenseman
WD = Weak-side defenseman
W = Wing
RW = Right wing
LW = Left wing
CT = Center
RS = Right-handed shot
LS = Left-handed shot
X = Defensive team
O = Offensive team
P = Player
C = Coach
○ = Shaded circle outline shows subsequent location of player
◉ = Puck
1 = Number of shot or pass
△ = Cone

Introduction

by coauthor Aaron Foeste

I've played ice hockey almost my entire life and haven't missed a season since I was 10 years old. I was pretty good and even played my last competitive season on our state-champion high school team. However, I wasn't quite good enough for prime time. I went directly from early morning peewee games to midnight face-offs in the adult league without ever seeing a skating rink in daylight. I always wondered, What do you have to do to play at 7:30 P.M. on Friday and Saturday nights? These are the sacred time slots allocated to groups of 40 elite players and the thousands of fans who pack huge arenas to watch them—while the local rinks host public skating sessions.

I've finally had the chance to ask this question—not once, but many times. Not to my buddies while we watched an NHL game, but to the top NCAA Division I coaches in the game. I asked the coaches who pick the NHL's future superstars from their high school and junior league teams and teach them how to compete for the first time in the national spotlight. These coaches devote months to watching amateur games to recruit a handful of select young players. Their coaching careers have been made by their ability to not only spot future talent but also transform players from local leagues into the players we all aspire to be. In other words, I had the opportunity to finally ask the people who could give me a real answer.

All the coaches I interviewed run extremely successful instructional camps and regularly attend countless youth-league games, yet they can be seen every Friday and Saturday night coaching some of the world's top players at North America's NCAA Division I schools such as Harvard University, Dartmouth College, the University of Connecticut, and Yale University. They comprise a small, highly specialized group of instructors who bridge the gap between two very different worlds—the leagues we all play in and the leagues we all watch. It is very rare in sports to find this niche, where coaches move seamlessly between these groups and are in the position to transport select players across this divide. Clearly, these are the coaches we want to train us and instruct us on the finer points of the game.

In the first chapter, these coaches, led by coauthor Rand Pecknold, head coach of the Quinnipiac University men's ice hockey team, offer their insights about the skills required for elite hockey. The information in this chapter gave me, a lifelong hockey player, a totally different view of the game; I was surprised that I was surprised by so much of what the coaches said.

The first chapter outlines a foundation of skills and concepts that are needed in the highest levels of hockey, and each of the following chapters is devoted to providing the most innovative, proven techniques to practice and acquire these skills. In addition to providing practice techniques, the insights of these coaches will change the way you see and think about the game. Better yet, they offer you the chance to see the game the way an experienced coach and recruiter sees it. They teach the nuances that separate the best from the very good. For example, the point isn't to teach you how to shoot or where to aim the puck, but how and why you should change the release point of your shot or develop the toe drag to throw off the defender's timing before you shoot. The final chapter is targeted to coaches who are committed to teaching hockey skills and strategy most efficiently, whether it is at the Squirt C level or a top prep school.

Coaches

In addition to coauthoring this book, Rand Pecknold assembled a formidable team of coaches to contribute to it.

Rand Pecknold (Head Coach, Quinnipiac University)

Rand Pecknold is one of hockey's greatest examples of a teaching and a player development coach. He advanced Quinnipiac University's men's ice hockey program from Division II obscurity to elite status as an Eastern College Athletic Conference (ECAC) Division I contender after becoming its head coach 15 years ago. Twenty-two of his players have graduated into the professional ranks during Quinnipiac's climb. And he runs youth-development camps that have more than 1,200 registrants annually. Along the way, Pecknold has racked up some very impressive credentials, including:

- Ninth among active Division I coaches in win percentage (.620)
- All-time winningest coach in Quinnipiac hockey history (263)
- Atlantic Hockey Coach of the Year in 2005
- Twenty-two Quinnipiac players have advanced into professional hockey during his tenure
- Twenty-one Quinnipiac players have been named All-League, nine have been named All-Rookie, five have been League Player of the Year, and five have been League Rookie of the Year
- Four Quinnipiac players have been All-Americans, and one has been named a Hobey Baker Award Finalist

Pecknold's place, as well as that of Quinnipiac's program, is solidified in college hockey's ultracompetitive NCAA Division I, where Quinnipiac's schedule includes regular televised games against the

University of Michigan (nine national titles), the University of Wisconsin (six national titles), and Harvard University (one national title). In addition to his achievements in coaching, Pecknold earned a B.A. in Economics and a Master's degree in Education from Connecticut College, where he played varsity ice hockey.

Bruce Marshall (Head Coach, University of Connecticut)

In his 20 seasons at the helm of the Connecticut men's ice hockey program, Bruce Marshall has led the Huskies to the Metro Atlantic Athletic Conference (MAAC) Championship final game once and to the semifinals of the MAAC Championship twice, as well as to three MAAC quarterfinal games, one Atlantic Hockey quarterfinal game, eight ECAC East tournament berths, four ECAC semifinals, and one ECAC championship appearance. Marshall's career record stands at 272–262–52 (.509). Marshall's tenure as head coach has marked the winningest period in Husky hockey history.

Marshall has been recognized by his peers by winning the Edward Jeremiah College Division National Coach of the Year Award, and he was named the ECAC Coach of the Year in 1992. In 1993, Marshall was named to the East squad coaching staff for the 1993 Shrine East-West College Hockey Classic. This was the first honor of its kind to be bestowed upon a Connecticut hockey coach.

Marshall was a four-year letter winner at Connecticut, and, in 1985, his team became the first Connecticut ice hockey team to make the ECAC playoffs. Marshall serves as a staff member for numerous clinics and camps in the area and as the Director of Connecticut Hockey Experience.

Frank Serratore (Head Coach, Air Force)

Frank Serratore has been head coach of the Air Force Falcons for the past 13 years. The Falcons had their best season ever in 2007–08, winning a school-record 21 Division I games and 14 league games. They also won the Atlantic Hockey Association (AHA) tournament championship for the second straight year and earned a back-to-back NCAA tournament appearance. The Falcons took home two all-conference honors and three all-tournament honors. Serratone is the only coach in Air Force Academy history to lead the team to five consecutive 15-win seasons and 19 or more wins in consecutive seasons.

Serratore came to the Academy from the Manitoba Moose, where he was the director of hockey operations, head coach, and general manager. Prior to that, he was the head coach at the University of Denver, coach and general manager of the Omaha Lancers (USHL), assistant coach at the University of North Dakota, and head coach and general manager of the Rochester Mustangs (USHL) and of the Austin Mavericks (USHL).

Serratore attended Western Michigan University from 1977–79 before completing his playing career at Bemidji State University in 1982. He played two seasons for the St. Paul Vulcans (USHL). In 2003 he was the head coach of the United States Under-17 Team that won the gold medal at the Five Nations Tournament in Prievizda, Slovakia. He has coached at two USA Hockey Olympic Sports Festivals and has been the coach of the USA Hockey Development Program since 1985. He is a member of the NCAA Championships Committee and has also been active on the Hobey Baker Selection Committee.

Ted Donato (Head Coach, Harvard University)

In his three seasons at Harvard, Donato has led his alma mater to its first back-to-back 20-win seasons since 1993–94, captured ECAC Hockey League and Ivy League championships, claimed two NCAA tournament berths, and coached two All-Americans. He has set new standards for wins by a Harvard coach in his first season and first three seasons.

Donato won an NCAA championship as a Crimson player, played in the Olympics, and enjoyed a 13-year NHL career. As an undergraduate, he finished his career 11th on the Crimson's career scoring chart (50 goals, 94 assists, 144 points) and remains 12th in that category. He earned All-ECAC and All-Ivy League accolades while serving as the 95th captain of Harvard Hockey in his 1990–91 senior season. As a member of the 1992 Olympic team, he tied for the team lead in scoring with four goals and three assists in eight games. He also played in the World Championships in 1997 (4–2–6 in eight games) and 1999 (2–6–8 in eight games) and in the 1988 World Junior Championships (3–2–5 in seven games). During his 13-year professional career, he played for the New York Rangers, the New York Islanders, the Los Angeles Kings, the Ottawa Senators, the Anaheim Ducks, and the St. Louis Blues.

Seth Appert (Head Coach, Rensselaer Polytechnic Institute)

Seth Appert is in his third season as the head coach of the men's ice hockey program at Rensselaer. Prior to that, Appert spent nine seasons as an assistant coach at the University of Denver, where he individually coached one All-American, two All-WCHA honorees, two WCHA Playoff Most Valuable Players, and two Frozen Four Most Outstanding Players at Denver. Three of his goaltenders were draft picks of the National Hockey League, one of whom was a Hobey Baker Award finalist.

While in Denver, he also coached or recruited the 2006 Hobey Baker Award winner, 8 All-Americans, 1 WCHA Player of the Year, 22 All-WCHA picks, 3 WCHA Defensive Players of the Year, 2 WCHA Student-Athletes of the Year, and 17 NHL draft picks. The Pioneers averaged over 23 wins per year during his tenure as an assistant coach and captured two NCAA National Championships, three WCHA Playoff Championships, and two WCHA regular-season titles. Coach Appert was a four-year letter winner at Ferris State from 1992–96.

Brian Daccord (Goaltending Consultant)

Brian Daccord is a former goaltending coach of the Boston Bruins. Daccord was on the staff of Stanley Cup–winning coaches Pat Burns and Mike Keenan as well as Robbie Ftorek. Daccord's book, *Hockey Goaltending*, has sold more than 30,000 copies worldwide, and he was featured in *The Hockey News* as one of the NHL's top goalie coaches with "crease clout." His current clients include top NHL, AHL, ECHL, college, and junior goalies. Daccord operates Stop It Goaltending, which conducts goalie camps and clinics as well as private training sessions for youth and elite goaltenders. Daccord is also a former coach and player at Merrimack College (NCAA Division I Hockey East) and played seven seasons of professional hockey in Switzerland. He has coached at every level of youth hockey; has been the coach for U.S. prep school, junior, college, and professional teams; is a Masters Level Coach with USA Hockey; and holds a Master's degree in Sports Science. Daccord is also the director of the Goaltending Consultant Group (GCG), made up of many of the top goalie coaches across North America. He is joined by other GCG consultants on the "Between the Pipes with Brian Daccord" segment of the "Inside Hockey" show aired weekly on XM Satellite and Sirius Radio. *Goalies' World Magazine* is where you can find Daccord's "Ask the Coach" column each issue, and he also writes a weekly blog for the fasthockey.com website.

Rick Bennett (Associate Head Coach, Union College)

Eric (Rick) Bennett begins his fourth season with the Union College Dutchmen in 2008 after spending the previous five years as an assistant coach at Providence College.

In addition to playing professional hockey for the Minnesota North Stars and the New York Rangers, Bennett was a 1990 graduate of Providence. There he ranked 21st in all-time scoring with 134 points (50 goals, 84 assists), earned Second-Team All-American honors as a junior, earned Second-Team All-Hockey East accolades as a senior captain, and was a Hobey Baker Award finalist. Bennett was also named to the Hockey East All-Freshman Team in 1987.

Kyle Wallack (Assistant Coach, Yale University)

Kyle Wallack was named an assistant coach for the Yale men's hockey team in June 2006. Prior to this, he was part of the Holy Cross coaching staff. Before Holy Cross, Wallack spent two seasons assisting the University of Connecticut men's squad, where he was recruiting coordinator and mentor to goalies. His Division I college career began at Quinnipiac in 1999.

Wallack's goaltending protégés include Holy Cross's Atlantic Hockey Goalie of the Year Tony Quesada and Connecticut's Atlantic Hockey All-Rookie Team Scott Tomes and Quinnipiac's Atlantic Hockey Goalie of the Year Jamie Holden. He also supervised Quinnipiac's Justin Eddy, who signed as a free agent with the Washington Capitals.

Michael Barrett (Former Head Coach, Quinnipiac University Women's Ice Hockey)

Mike Barrett spent six years as head coach of the Quinnipiac University women's hockey team. Prior to Quinnipiac, Barrett spent two years as head coach at Sacred Heart University. During the 2001–02 season, he guided the Pioneers to a 17–9 record. Sacred Heart also won the ECAC Open Championship that season.

Barrett played hockey for four seasons at Quinnipiac (1981–85). He finished his career with 126 points (62 goals, 64 assists), placing him 6th in goals, tied for 9th in points, and tied for 16th in assists, resulting in a ranking of third all-time in points and goals. As a result, he was inducted into the Quinnipiac Athletic Hall of Fame in 1990.

Dave Peters (Assistant Coach, Dartmouth College)

Dave Peters enters his ninth season as an assistant coach at Dartmouth College, where his team has had four consecutive winning seasons and has made four straight trips to the ECAC Championships.

Prior to coming to Dartmouth, Peters was the head coach and general manager of the Danville Wings Junior Hockey Team, top assistant at Providence College, assistant coach at Kent State, head coach at North Quincy, and assistant coach at Weymouth North, as well as coaching high school hockey in Massachusetts.

Coach Peters is widely considered to be one of the top assistant coaches in college hockey.

John Riley (Amateur Scout, Philadelphia Flyers)

John Riley is currently an amateur scout for the Philadelphia Flyers of the National Hockey League. He also serves as the head Eastern scout for the U.S. National Team Development Program. From 2005–2007 he was an assistant coach at Princeton University, and prior to that he was the head coach at Brunswick School in Connecticut. Since 1991 he has been a coach in the Player Development Program for the Atlantic District of USA Hockey, while also serving as the associate director of that program since 1999.

Ben Syer (Associate Head Coach, Quinnipiac University)

Ben Syer was named Quinnipiac University's men's ice hockey associate head coach this past summer after serving on the Bobcats' coaching staff for the previous nine seasons. The Bobcats have posted a stellar 189–117–32 (.607) record since Syer joined the Quinnipiac staff. He has directly recruited or assisted in recruiting individuals from the United States and Canada, where he has pursued some of the nation's top scholastic and junior talent.

Quinnipiac reached the MAAC tournament semifinals in each of the first four years of Syer's tenure, including three straight MAAC finals appearances. Included in that span were the 2002 MAAC tournament title and the first NCAA appearance in program history. The Bobcats also won the MAAC regular-season title in Syer's first year at Quinnipiac. Syer also helped guide Quinnipiac to the 2006–07 ECAC Hockey Tournament Championship game.

In his time with the Bobcats, Syer has coached five 100-point scorers, three ECAC Hockey all-tournament selections, and two ECAC Hockey Rookie of the Years in Bryan Leitch and Brandon Wong. In addition, Syer played a major role in the recruiting and development of three-time All-American Reid Cashman.

A native of Kitchener, Ontario, Syer arrived at Quinnipiac after serving one season as an assistant coach at Ohio University. At Ohio, Syer assisted with practice and game preparation as well as recruiting. He also earned a Master's degree in Physical Education with a concentration in Athletic Administration in June 2000.

A 1998 graduate of Western Ontario University, Syer earned a Bachelor's degree in Urban Development. He also has prior coaching experience with the North Middlesex Stars, a junior development team based in Parkhill, Ontario.

Scott Robson (Assistant Coach, Western Michigan University)

Scott Robson was recently named to the coaching staff at Western Michigan University after spending the previous six years as part of Rand Pecknold's coaching staff at Quinnipiac University. Robson, Pecknold's first recruiting commitment at Quinnipiac, has emerged as a top young coach after a fine playing career.

In his years as a coach with the Bobcats, the team posted a mark of 145–97–22 (.591). Quinnipiac won two MAAC regular-season championships and reached two MAAC Hockey League tournament finals during that span.

From 1999–2001, he was an assistant coach with the Valley Junior Warriors of the Eastern Junior Hockey League (EJHL). The position catapulted Robson into the general manager/head coach position with the Bay State Breakers (EJHL) for the 2001–02 season. With the Breakers, Robson was in charge of hockey and all business operations. He also led the team to its best record in league history. Robson coached several players who moved on to play Division I college hockey or professionally.

Robson finished his playing career with 77 points (28 goals, 49 assists) in just 90 games. At the time of his graduation, Robson ranked seventh on the school's all-time assist chart. After completing his playing career at Quinnipiac, Robson moved into an assistant coach's role for the 1998–99 season.

Bill Riga (Assistant Coach, Quinnipiac University)

Bill Riga joined the Quinnipiac University men's ice hockey staff for the 2008–09 season after serving as an assistant coach at ECAC Hockey rival Union College for the previous five seasons. While at Union, Riga served as the Dutchmen's primary recruiter, helping Union to their highest finish in their Division I history when all four of his previous recruiting classes played together in 2007–08. In his five years on staff at Union, the Dutchmen reached the ECAC Hockey tournament four times.

Prior to Union, Riga was the recruiting coordinator and associate head coach for the Boston Junior Bruins of the EJHL from 1996 to 2003, and 33 of his players signed Letters of Intent to Division I programs. From 2000 to 2002, Riga was also the head coach and director of hockey at the Rivers School in Weston, Massachusetts.

Riga was a four-year letter winner at Hockey East member University of Massachusetts–Lowell. In his time there, Riga helped the River Hawks to four Hockey East tournament semifinal appearances and two NCAA tournament quarterfinal appearances. Riga was also a Hockey East All-Academic selection and the recipient of the 1996 Gus Coutu Award for exemplifying the spirit of UMass Lowell men's ice hockey.

Duncan Fletcher (Professional Athlete Transition Institute)

Duncan Fletcher is currently the director of the Professional Athlete Transition Institute at Quinnipiac University, which manages the Life After Hockey program for the NHL, NHL Alumni, and the NHL Players' Association. He is a former assistant hockey coach at Quinnipiac. Before coaching at Quinnipiac, he was a player-development specialist and recruiter for the Victoria Salsa in the British Columbia Junior Hockey League. He has had several players go on to careers in the NHL.

The Quinnipiac men's hockey team versus Holy Cross at the TD Banknorth Sports Center, Quinnipiac University
Courtesy of QuinnipiacBobcats.com

1
What Do Recruiters Look For?

Before you work on developing highly specialized skills, you need to have a big-picture understanding of the game of hockey and how you want to progress through your season—and your playing career. With a clear understanding of where you want to go and how to get there, the drills and strategies in this book will make much more sense. To many fans and players, hockey looks like a rapid and very chaotic, but highly entertaining, collection of random events: a mad scramble by quickly alternating groups of players for a puck they can barely keep track of. As you develop your "hockey sense," however, the rhythms and flow of the game will begin to appear and the chaos will be replaced by purposeful systems and complex strategies that make sense. That's when the real fun begins.

The combination of understanding the game and its rhythms and of making the connection between cause and effect is what coaches call hockey sense. Hockey sense is frequently mentioned by coaches as one of the most important factors in a player's success. Lack of it, more than anything else, holds players back, while "getting it" propels them forward.

In spite of how important it is, hockey sense is difficult to describe and to quantify. Occasionally, a player or coach puts a concept into words that, for the first time, explains how or why something happens. Prior to this explanation, we could see the result but not associate the cause. Perhaps the best example is Wayne Gretzky's famous explanation about how he came up with so many loose pucks and was always in the right position. He said he skated to where the puck is *going* to be, not to where it *is*. It's so simple—and the perfect answer to the question of why he was always in the right place at the right time—but nobody had ever said it like that before.

Now players have one aspect of his greatness distilled into a simple concept they can follow as they are skating: where the puck is going to be. Even better, they can cause the puck to go to a certain place by doing something even when they don't have it. This statement has become part of the collective consciousness of players and coaches and has altered how they think about the game, about playing styles, and about how to teach strategy.

The next question would obviously be how to teach and practice skating to where the puck is going to be. Unless you get the big-picture concept or have developed hockey sense, practicing forechecking systems that are designed to force the opposing team to move the puck to the area where *your team* wants it to go will seem like confusing and meaningless skating patterns during practice.

One of best ways to encourage hockey sense is to have individuals with a highly developed sense of the game—some of college hockey's best coaches, for example—explain in their own words how they see the game, player development, and training. These coaches' comments will offer many new insights for those of you who are strategizing and planning your progression into elite hockey. In addition, for many players, the process of moving up and figuring out what it will take to "get there" is a mystery. You know you have to be good, but you may not be exactly sure of what that means. To take the mystery out of the process, we asked several coaches who spend countless hours recruiting new players for their college hockey programs what they look for in recruits to whom they will make an offer to advance into a NCAA Division I program. We then went a step further and asked several questions about how to—or how not to—train and develop the skills necessary to get chosen by an elite team.

What Coaches Want

The following five questions were the basis for our discussions with the coaches. The subsequent chapters teach the skills and the hockey sense that is needed, according to these top coaches, to compete at the highest levels of hockey.

Rand Pecknold, Quinnipiac University
Courtesy of QuinnipiacBobcats.com

1. When recruiting players for your Division I program, what are the top three attributes you look for in a player before you make him or her an offer?
2. Once they are on your team, what skills or strategy do you find that you most often have to teach new recruits in order for them to be competitive at the Division I level?
3. What should a player concentrate on most to create a foundation of skills and knowledge that can most effectively be built upon to move to higher levels of play?

4. Are there any common examples of mistakes that you can attribute to ineffective coaching, training, or strategy, rather than to a lack of coaching?

5. In the past five years, what has changed most in what you teach or how you coach?

Responses from the Coaches

In cases where coaches had very similar responses for one or more of the questions, the answers are not repeated. In other words, it is not the case that coaches didn't answer all of the questions; rather, I've eliminated overlaps. And, as the author, I included my top five attributes in my first answer, even though only three are requested!

Rand Pecknold, Quinnipiac University

When recruiting players for your Division I program, what are the top three attributes you look for in a player before you make him an offer?

1. Talent in skating, stickhandling, and shooting
2. Hockey sense
3. Competitiveness
4. Character
5. Commitment to academics

• **Talent.** I look for raw skating and basic hockey skills. I first evaluate players on their straight-ahead, north-south skating speed. Then I look at east-west skating agility and balance. How many steps does it take a player to get up to full speed? Some players aren't as fast as others in straight skating, but if they can get up to top speed in one or two steps, it makes a big difference. I'm also looking for players that have that "extra gear"—the ones who can turn it up when you think they're already at top speed. These are the players who get the defensive player thinking he's got the play timed and then blow by him.

You've got to have a hard shot to play college or pro, that's a given, and everybody in those leagues can blast the puck. What sets them apart from the players who didn't move up is their range of shots (backhand, wrist, slap, and snap—they're all great); how quickly they can release the shot; and, lastly, accuracy—not just hitting the net, but picking corners and making the goalie work on every shot they take.

- **Hockey sense.** I need to see players demonstrate an ability to anticipate the play. Like Gretzky said, it's more important to go where the puck (or play) is going to be, rather than where it is or has been. At Quinnipiac, we can teach systems for forechecking,

Ben Nelson, Quinnipiac University   Courtesy of QuinnipiacBobcats.com backchecking, the power play, etc., but I ultimately need players to know where to go when they don't have the puck—in or out of the context of a system. Hockey sense can't really be taught, it has to develop, and I recruit only players with a highly developed hockey sense. Players who can step up to the next level are proactive, rather than reactive. They're also patient. When I see a player panic with the puck or get rid of it too quickly, without purpose, I know his hockey sense isn't fully developed. I want to see patience, poise, and purposeful movement of the puck.

• **Competitiveness.** A player's on- and off-ice performance both give me a good idea of his level of competitiveness. What challenges has the player taken on in his life, which extracurricular activities is he involved in, what types of classes does he take, and has he been successful in these areas? Competitiveness is a critical trait in elite hockey. Whether it's late in the third period of a big game and there's a battle in the corner for the puck, or it's late in the summer and players are in the weight room, the top players want to win and are focused on winning. A player has to have a strong, competitive personality to compete at this level. On the ice, I can often see competitiveness more clearly when the player is not near the puck. For example, is he skating as hard as he can to cover the opponent; how fast is he skating to get back into the play; and is he battling in front of the net for the coveted slot area?

• **Character.** I summarize character as, "Doing the right thing when nobody is looking." Character is very important in college and pro hockey for several reasons. We're making a big investment in our players and are counting on them to do the right thing. Character doesn't just mean staying out of trouble. Character gets you to the weight room and off-ice training over the summer when there's no supervision from the coach. The top players are dedicated to training, and a lack of character is going to result in cutting corners in training. I choose my captains based on the example they set off of the ice, and it always translates to on-ice performance.

• **Commitment to academics.** All college coaches have gone through the nightmare of having a starting player's eligibility jeopardized by academic problems, and we are all looking to avoid that problem going forward. Most people probably expect a coach to list commitment to academics as one of his top priorities just to keep the athletic director at his school happy, but it really is one of the top criteria used in evaluating recruits. We spend so many hours together every week that no one wants to have a player who creates a lot of trouble around, even if he's got a great shot compared to the other potential recruits in his junior league. The adjustment to adult-student-athlete is very difficult (in fact, adjusting to any one of those three is difficult), and a poor student is not going to be able to make the jump to the next level of academics, especially when combined with the schedule and pressures of competing at the Division I level.

Dave Peters, Dartmouth College

When recruiting players for your Division I program, what are the top three attributes you look for in a player before you make him an offer?

- **Intelligence and hockey sense.** When I'm recruiting, I like to sit as high as possible in the stands. I can see the entire ice, who's open, and when a play should be made or a shot taken. I can see if a player can anticipate the play, for example, passing to the area his teammate will be in next to set up the play. Three-on-twos and two-on-ones are also a great way for me to judge a player's hockey sense: it's very clear in these situations if the defensive players know how to play it, if the puck-carrier can read the play, and if the other forwards can get open to set up the play.
- **Competitiveness.** My favorite way to measure competitiveness is with loose pucks. For example, how many times does a player go into the corner and come out with the puck?
- **Ability to improve.** I'm not always looking for the best high school or junior player—I'm looking for the one who will be the best in four to six years. There are many great college programs

that may not be the first choice of the top players. This is a great advantage to most student-athletes when they are being recruited for college sports. Many programs won't focus on the top high school player in the country because the coaches know the probability of recruiting that player is low. This shifts the focus of most college recruiters to a potential player's attitude, work ethic, grades, and ability to improve. I think the notion that players don't have to come in with good academic records is just not true. Most coaches I know of don't want to go through the headache of dealing with a recruit's academic problems once he is in the program. Perhaps a few of the top players in any given year aren't the greatest students, but for the rest, a great academic record is a huge positive factor in deciding to make an offer to a player to come up to a Division I program.

Once they are on your team, what skills or strategy do you find that you most often have to teach new recruits in order for them to be competitive at the Division I level?

There are three things that require big adjustments for our new players. I can't say that we have something specific to teach in every situation, but I'll list the factors that require the greatest transitions.

- **Strength**—especially during the season
- **Pace.** The speed and pace of the game is so much faster, there's a lot less time and space than even the best new players are used to—that's why hockey sense is so important when moving up to the next level.
- **Off ice.** Players are away from home for the first time, and there's a big mental adjustment to not only starting college, but to playing a sport at one of the most elite levels, with all of the adjustments that any young man or woman has to make when starting college.

Rick Bennett, Union College

When recruiting players for your Division I program, what are the top three attributes you look for in a player before you make him an offer?

- **Hockey sense.** I'm looking for playmaking ability—reading the situation, making the right pass, moving to the right area, working out of a tight space. Whether this ability is learned or natural, a player needs to be at the top of the pack in terms of hockey sense if he's going to be able to compete at the next level up.
- **Character.** Academics are at the top of the list. I think other coaches are going to say this as well; a player really has to be a student first if he's planning to play college hockey. Character is what gives him the discipline to make it to the library as well as the rink or the weight room.
- **Skating.** Based on how important skating is to hockey and how many players I see on recruiting trips who make it through more than 10 years of youth hockey and are weak in one or more aspects of their skating, I highly recommend power-skating schools.

Once they are on your team, what skills or strategy do you find that you most often have to teach new recruits in order for them to be competitive at the Division I level?

- **Shooting to score.** The goalies are so good and so much faster than they are in the leagues below, that a player is not going to score if he simply puts the puck on the net. This surprises a lot of our new players who were high scorers on their high school teams, where, because of their really hard shots, they could count on scoring a lot of goals just by keeping their shots on net. At our level, you've got to take every shot like it's your last. You've got to put everything you have into it, in terms of both speed and placement. You literally have to shoot to score, and once you're here, you can count on facing very highly trained, talented goalies for the rest of your career.

- **Defensive-zone systems.** A lot of players have to work on making the transition to a more dynamic defensive-zone system. Rather than simply cover-your-man, we have to teach head-on-a-swivel vision to pick up players and pick up on developing plays. There's a lot more collapsing together of the five players and then branching out again, rather than a linear system of staying in your assigned area at all times. I'd summarize this by adding that communication is a much bigger part of our games than I think it is where the new players are coming from. The game moves so much faster, and we rely on constant talking.

What should a player concentrate on most to create a foundation of skills and knowledge that can most effectively be built upon to move to higher levels of play?

Like I said before, I'd like to see much more dedication to becoming great skaters, rather than racking up more trips to tournaments or playing extra games. Players should attend a power-skating clinic before it's too late.

Are there any common examples of mistakes that you can attribute to ineffective coaching, training, or strategy, rather than to a lack of coaching?

I think there is way too much emphasis on tournaments. For the same time and money, players could attend a power-skating school and get the chance to work on what is keeping a lot of players out of the college leagues—skating. A specialized camp is also a much better use of time and money, especially when you have access to college or pro coaches at the camps, who know what you need to know to move up and can teach it. I think it's good to experience a variety of coaching styles as you progress though hockey, and a camp is one of the best ways to do this.

In the past five years, what has changed most in what you teach or how you coach?

There are a lot of great new training techniques for stickhandling and shooting, especially off-ice practice time with stick. For example, stickhandling golf balls or stickhandling golf balls with the front half of the stick blade sawn off. A golf ball is great for overspeed stick training—it's faster than a puck or roller hockey ball. Some players use glasses with blinders that keep them from seeing down. Shoot and pass heavy pucks, both on the ice and off. This develops strength and stick-speed needed for high velocity shots. Just don't practice slap shots with the lead pucks though; they can be bad for your wrists— and your stick.

Michael Barrett, Quinnipiac University (Women's)

When recruiting players for your Division I program, what are the top three attributes you look for in a player before you make her an offer?

- **Skating.** I'm assessing speed and style—looking for length of stride and quickness.
- **Good hands.** I want to see a player stickhandle though traffic and make hard tape-to-tape passes in traffic.
- **Work ethic.** I'll summarize this as stop-and-go, in other words, no circling back into the play.

Once they are on your team, what skills or strategy do you find that you most often have to teach new recruits in order for them to be competitive at the Division I level?

- **Skating.** We have to convince them to go back to work on basics and to learn new concepts.
- **Systems.** Forechecking, backchecking, etc. all need a lot of work to transition to a full-team system that we use in Division I.

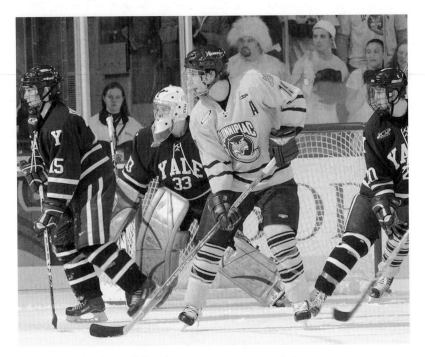

Jamie Bates, Quinnipiac University   Courtesy of QuinnipiacBobcats.com

Bruce Marshall, University of Connecticut

When recruiting players for your Division I program, what are the top three attributes you look for in a player before you make him an offer?

• **The ability to create opportunities, to make good decisions quickly, and to handle the puck under pressure**—especially defensive players when required to make a good first breakout pass under pressure.

• **Work ethic.** I assess work ethic by how a player plays when he is away from the puck, not when he has it. In particular, is he alert at all times, and what is his demeanor and level of discipline on the ice?

Ted Donato, Harvard University

When recruiting players for your Division I program, what are the top three attributes you look for in a player before you make him an offer?

When we recruit we look for players with that unique combination of superior academics and outstanding hockey talent. From a hockey perspective, we look for players who can skate and handle the puck at this level, players who have a high "hockey IQ," and players who we feel have "upside." Last, and most important, we look for players with outstanding character who understand the incredible opportunities Harvard affords and who embrace the history and tradition of excellence that are associated with Harvard Hockey.

Kyle Wallack, Yale University

When recruiting players for your Division I program, what are the top three attributes you look for in a player before you make him an offer?

Recruiting is a major emphasis of every college hockey program. Bringing to campus student-athletes with immeasurable character levels will make for a highly successful learning environment. At Yale, each of these athletes must be highly motivated individuals, both on the ice and in the classroom. Our goal is to identify the top student-athletes in the world.

Once we have identified the academic side of the student-athlete, we focus more on the hockey side. The four main things we look for in our players are:

1. Character
2. Skill level
3. Skating
4. Competitiveness

We feel that bringing in top-level-character kids who are competitive, talented, and good citizens will make us succeed at the Division I level.

Frank Serratore, Air Force

When recruiting players for your Division I program, what are the top three attributes you look for in a player before you make him an offer?

At the Air Force Academy, we provide our student-athletes with a tremendous package, which includes a highly accredited degree program, a full financial aid package, a guaranteed job after graduation, and the opportunity of competing at the NCAA Division I level. With this, however, we are required to operate under a very strict set of guidelines in recruiting potential student-athletes. We must look for good players who are good citizens, good students, and U.S. or dual U.S. citizens. Also, these prospects cannot possess any major medical flaws such as asthma, diabetes, and so on. If any one of these criteria is not met, we cannot recruit the student-athlete in question. The most difficult part of the recruiting process is locating good players who fit all the criteria. We define a good player as one who possesses at least one Division I attribute. In building our team, we realize we are not going to acquire a player or group of players who "have it all." However, by recruiting players who each bring a piece of the puzzle to the table, we will ultimately obtain all the pieces needed to be successful within the collective framework of our team.

Another obstacle we face is the fact that the majority of people we recruit do not come from military backgrounds. Thus they possess preconceptions about the academy environment. Once they visit our campus and experience the environment firsthand, most admit their initial perceptions were far from reality and they become even more interested. Subsequently, once we locate such a candidate and fully educate him and his parents on the program, we are typically successful in securing a commitment. Interestingly enough, virtually every one of the players in our present locker room never really thought about or considered a service academy prior to our staff making contact; however, we identified certain characteristics within each of these people that indicated to us they had the attributes needed to succeed in our environment.

In conclusion, I believe every athletic program must possess a culture. Success in recruiting comes from pursuing people who fit what you are. I also feel there needs to be a parallel between the culture of your athletic program and the culture of your school. Remember, as a recruiter you are not just recruiting a prospect as an athlete; you are recruiting a prospect as a student-athlete. Too often, recruiters simply pursue who they feel are the best players available. I can tell you, without question, the "best players" available to the Air Force Academy may not necessarily be the right players. We have been successful by pursuing players who we feel fit our culture. It is no coincidence that the right type of players for our hockey program mirrors the right type of people for the academy, and ultimately, these are the types of individuals who evolve over time into great Air Force officers.

Seth Appert, Rensselaer Polytechnic Institute

When recruiting players for your Division I program, what are the top three attributes you look for in a player before you make him an offer?

- **Competitiveness.** It's hard to quantify competitiveness, but I know it when I see it. For example, when two players go into the corner for a loose puck, they should have an equal chance of getting it. There are players who come out with the puck 70 percent of the time, though, game after game. Once I've been to see a player several times and I don't think it's 50/50 anymore that he's going to come up with the loose puck—but I assume he's going to get it because I've seen him do it so many times—then I want that player on my team.

Dave Peters, Dartmouth (Goaltending)

What are the most important attributes you seek in a goalie?

- **Find it/see it/stop it.**
- **Lateral agility, mobility, and explosiveness.** Not goal line to blue line, but behind the net, post-to-post, short bursts within the crease: the goalie must be a great skater in a small space— his space in and around the crease.

What qualities and obstacles do goalies face when they join a Division I program?

Knowing what it takes to transition from high school hockey to elite Division I college hockey can help players at all levels, not just those actually making this transition. I think it's very helpful to know what challenges players at the highest skill levels face so that you can best prepare yourself physically and mentally to make the jump to the next highest level of play, no matter where you are playing now. For some players, just having someone put these concepts into words makes all the difference.

New goalies on Division I teams are most likely one of the top players from the league they were in the previous year. As a result, they probably are in the habit of "checking out" or taking time off mentally during games and still being successful. Also, the Division I schedule is shorter, but much more intense, than most high school or junior schedules. In other words, each of our games counts a lot more toward getting to the national tournament because we have a relatively short schedule. The games are much more intense and often covered in the national media. A goalie can't take any mental vacations during games or training, and this is one of the more difficult adjustments for new goaltenders.

Some other specific adjustments include:

- Ability to control rebounds and get into position for the second save
- Speed of game: adjusting to much faster passes, shots, and transitions to the next play
- Due to new rules, goalie equipment is now smaller, and more interference penalties are being called. The result is more passing and more shots with less equipment space covering the net—the hybrid goalie style.

Brian Daccord (Goaltending)

What are the most important attributes you seek in a goalie?

- A goalie who is alert at all times: is he making breakout passes when the other team is changing lines, is he communicating to his teammates about positioning and directing traffic in front of his net, does he go right to the bench on a delayed penalty or is his mind out of the game? These are all examples of signals I pick up on when recruiting goalies.
- In my opinion, one of the most important attributes a goalie must have if he's going to advance is his determination to contest all shots—no matter how little of a chance he has to make the save. All goalies are going to work for the save that they have a 90 percent probability of making. On plays where everybody in the rink thinks it's going to be a goal, where there's maybe a 10 percent chance of making the save on the second or third shot, time after time I see goalies who assume it's going in and don't really work to make the save. The players I want on my team are the ones who work for every save. As you move up, the forwards just keep shooting faster and more accurately—the saves a goalies has

to work really hard for in his current league are going to be common in the next league up.

John Riley, Philadelphia Flyers Scout (Offense)

What do you believe makes for an effective offense?

While it can be argued that a highly skilled player or team will generate offense individually, a mid-lane drive or going to the net without the puck is the single most important element of an offensive attack and of the creation of goal-scoring opportunities. While perhaps it goes against conventional wisdom to think that a player *without* the puck can do more to create offense than a player *with* the puck, it is fairly natural when you consider that players spend 97 percent of their time without the puck on their stick. So since players have the puck so little of the time, a good offensive player should most often be doing something that will facilitate offense while not necessarily handling the puck. This is called "supporting the puck," and as the great Wayne Gretzky showed us, one should not skate to where the puck is but rather skate to where the puck is going to be. As the object of the sport is to put the puck in the net, it is only appropriate that if you don't have the puck you should skate to where it is going to be—the net!

What do you mean by "drive the net"?

Certainly there are different approaches you could take to answer this question. I think Jamie Fitzpatrick sums up the idea well with his definition: "An aggressive hockey strategy in which a forward charges toward the opponent's net in hopes of deflecting a shot, banging a loose puck, obstructing the goaltender's view, and simply creating mayhem that could lead to a scoring chance for his team." I could not have said it better myself!

Why go to the net?

There are a variety of reasons to go to the net. First, going to the net is an aggressive and proactive approach to offense. An offensive player

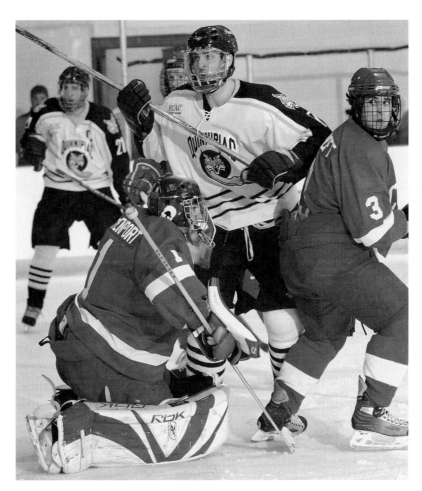

Don Travis, Quinnipiac University, driving the net versus Cornell
Courtesy of QuinnipiacBobcats.com

who does not have the puck should "move and create" rather than "watch and wait." By moving without the puck he will create time and space for the puck carrier (known as F1) to make a play. Additionally, as a player away from the puck drives the net, he will inevitably take a defensive player with him and, in doing so, create space behind him ("turn hard ice into soft ice") for the next offensive player (F3) to fill in.

Secondly, driving the net will break down the defensive team by creating a numerical advantage at the puck and, perhaps, away from the puck as well. (Think a miniature power play.) On a line rush, F2 can create a two-on-one by driving the net off the inside shoulder of the weak-side defenseman. This forces the weak-side defenseman to decide if he should go with F2 to the net front or stay high to protect the slot area that F3 is about to fill in. While the defending player is trying to decide which option to cover, the puck-carrier will likely have a moment to make a play. Further, even if the defenseman reacts well and makes a quick decision, the puck-carrier can read his choice and distribute the puck to the open teammate. (This assumes that F3 beats the defensive backcheckers into the soft ice.)

Additionally, by going to the net hard, F2 challenges the goaltender and makes his task of locating and stopping the puck more difficult. By charging the goal, offensive players will invariably force a goaltender to divert some of his attention to the bodies that are headed his way. This will obviously decrease his focus on the puck, which will naturally afford the offensive team a better chance of getting the puck past him. Think about it: a hockey puck weighs 6 ounces and an average 15-year-old weighs approximately 150 pounds—which one would you focus on if they were both coming at you?

Driving the net hard in hockey is analogous to a baseball player running hard from first to second on a 5-4-3 double-play ball. If the runner heads to second vigorously and slides, he will make the job of the second baseman harder, as he will invariably become concerned about his safety. This is universally accepted as a clean play and a part of good baseball. This same approach applies to a hockey player as he drives the net. F2 should be belligerent in his approach to the net. He should crash the net hard and see what happens. Collisions will most certainly occur, but they are part of the game. As Tom Renney, head coach of the New York Rangers, said following a 2008 playoff game with the New Jersey Devils in which the Rangers were accused of "running" Martin Brodeur: "That's how you play. That's how you win at this level. It's not to go after a goaltender. It's to go to the front of the net. It's a body-contact game, and that's the way it works out."

In playing an offense like you describe, is there a common philosophy to your attack, beyond being aggressive?

Regardless of your philosophy or scheme, triangulation is the key to success. This is not hockey exclusive. In basketball Phil Jackson has won nine NBA Championships with his lauded "triangle offense." In chess, the key to success is to control the middle of the board while having support on the wings. In war, in order to win a battle you need support on the flanks to contain the enemy.

For an offensive attack in hockey, F2 penetrates the front line of defense and pushes through, thereby creating soft ice for F3 to fill and be available for a pass from F1. This tactic is equally effective and the fundamental principles always remain the same whether off a line rush, from a turnover in the offensive zone, or off an offensive zone face-off. The message is always the same: Move the puck. Go to the net. Fill the space behind. Create a triangle!

Think of a water skier. The speedboat penetrates the rough water, flattening and smoothing it out, making a triangle directly behind the boat for the skier to cruise through. The skier can easily stay behind the boat in the soft water. Without the boat going through the area first, it would be very difficult to ski through the water. For our purposes, think of F2 as the boat: the boat is clearing out a lane for F3, the skier.

It seems like a simple concept, so what is the big deal?

"Simple, not easy" is a quote I learned from John Hynes, head coach of the USA Hockey national program, that best answers this question. He talks about hockey being simple but not easy to play. Going to the net is easy to talk about, but it is certainly not easy to do.

As an offensive player it is very easy to go for a drop pass or become F3 on a line rush. It is also very easy to defend, as the opposing defenseman is never forced to make a decision or move laterally. He can instead casually backskate his lane and maintain defensive side positioning without ever being put in a stressful situation. Additionally, the goaltender who is never challenged is free to track the puck without interference.

Conversely, it is not easy and in fact is very hard to be F2 and belligerently attack the net, all the while getting slashed, whacked, and otherwise beaten in the name of offense. This when most often you won't even get credited with an assist for your effort! However, when F2 takes this approach he is extremely difficult to defend, as the defensive player is forced to read and react, gap vertically and laterally, and engage physically while trying to track the puck. Most defenders put in this position will inevitably get caught guessing, sleeping, or cheating or simply become overwhelmed and very often get beat. The result is offense—and goals!

The key here is desire and commitment. As an offensive player, you are either willing to go to the net or you are not. You are either willing to pay the price or you are not. You are either willing to sacrifice your body or you are not. As one coach told me: "Think of the bacon, egg, and cheese sandwich. The chicken is involved, but the pig is committed." Be the pig! Be committed. Go to the net!

Can you explain what you mean by a transition line rush and how to attack the offensive zone?

This is somewhat theoretical, of course, because hockey is a chaotic game where the puck changes hands more than 400 times in a 60-minute game. However, if you look at a traditional three-on-two line rush, which happens fairly regularly in any given hockey game, the first collective thought should be to get the puck outside the face-off dots, in hopes of generating speed and width to the attack.

From there each attacking player has a specific responsibility:

- **F1 (puck-carrier):** Attack the offensive zone *wide* with *speed*. The first priority must be to gain the offensive zone and get through the gray zone (the area just inside the offensive blue line). Upon accomplishing this he should look for supporting players and always look to get the puck to the net.

- **F2:** Provide low puck support by driving to the net hard. He must penetrate the defenseman and work to get behind him. He should always drive on the puck side of the weak-side defenseman and set his sights on the endpoint—the net!

- **F3:** Provide high puck support by delaying and staying wide on the weak side and look to fill the soft ice created by F2 driving the net.

- **Defenseman:** Look to create a second wave of attack, or perhaps join the rush as F3 when appropriate. If this occurs, the puck-carrier will have multiple options:

  1. Shoot to score!
  2. Propel the puck toward the net—knowing there is a player going for a redirect, deflection, or rebound(s).
  3. Pass the puck to F3 or a defenseman who has filled soft ice in the slot area.
  4. Curl back (a.k.a. the Gretzky curl) toward the boards and look for a second wave (defenseman).
  5. Get the puck into the corner (cycle the puck) for F2, who is already in position to touch the puck first. F2 could come from the weak side or from the middle of the ice. Do not confuse "mid-lane drive" to mean only the middle forward. That being said, wherever he begins, F2 needs to be sure to cut in between the defenseman and drive on to the strong-side post!

What about a drop pass in this situation?

Ah, the dreaded drop pass! The drop pass will create an inverted triangle, which inevitably leads to a violation of all the rules of generating offense. When F2 goes behind the puck-carrier to receive the drop pass, he becomes reactive to the puck-carrier and is now watching the play rather than creating the play. By doing so, there is no penetration or mid-lane drive and zero pressure applied to the defenseman or goaltender.

Ultimately, the drop pass is very easy to defend, as the defensemen can easily skate their lanes and stay in the shooting alleys. Moreover, and perhaps most important, the drop pass most often occurs in the gray zone. This can be deadly and is a turnover waiting to happen. As a general rule, players should look to get the puck through the gray zone as quickly and cleanly as possible. The last thing a player should look to do in this spot is move the puck backward, or toward his own goal! There are times when a lateral takeover, or a cross and drop, is effective, but that is an entirely different option.

What about generating offense from a turnover in the offensive zone?

Generally speaking, the same rules apply:

- **F1 (puck-carrier):** Upon securing the puck on transition from defense/forecheck, the player should immediately get his head up and be sure to protect the puck. He was just given the puck—don't give it right back! Then he should find some open ice, hopefully toward the goal, and skate toward it.
- **F2:** Provide low support by driving to the net hard and get on the strong side of the ice. In all likelihood a defending player will go with him—and chase him to the net.
- **F3:** As is the case on the line rush, F3 should provide high support (complete the triangulation) by filtering into soft ice that was created by F2 going to the net.

How about generating offensive from a face-off?

A face-off is a 50/50 puck and a great opportunity to generate offense. First, it should be noted that winning the face-off is the responsibility of the entire team, and for the purpose of this discussion we will assume that the offensive team has won the draw. With this being the case, it is critical that, depending on the situation (for example, time of game, score, six-on-five), at least one forward drive the net as soon as the puck is won. The forward should look to beat his defender to the net and work to get in the shooting lane to block the vision of the goaltender. As the puck moves from low to high, the offensive defenseman should be sure to move the puck as quickly and accurately as possible. When looking to generate offense in this situation, the puck should go from low to high, and then it should move (shot or passed) as quickly as possible. Most important, upon the puck being propelled toward the net, there should already be a minimum of one forward at the goal mouth looking to redirect, deflect, or tip the puck and fight for rebounds should there be one.

You rely on your forwards for the aggressive play you describe. What fundamentals are key to stress to them?

Here are some simple buzz phrases that can be used for forwards of all ages:

- Obtain offensive side positioning (puck side of the player defending you).
- When driving the net you should work to turn the weak-side defenseman.
- Keep your stick on the ice!
- Fight through stick checks!
- You are entitled to that ice—keep your feet moving!
- Go to the blue! (The blue paint at the crease.)
- Don't skate past the net. Stop at the goal mouth!
- Get rebounds! Score ugly goals!

Additionally, these are thoughts from Dennis "Red" Gendron, who is currently the associate head coach at the University of Massachusetts:

General Rules for Forwards

1. Go to the net *with* and *without* the puck. It should be a forward's first thought, his first instinct.
2. From the half wall or the corner, beat your defender to the net.
3. Shoot the puck on net! Any shot is a good shot—particularly from the A scoring area!

2

Elite Skating and Stickhandling Skills

The basic elements of ice hockey—stickhandling, shooting, and skating—are usually covered in separate chapters in instructional books. To make it to the elite levels of hockey, however, requires that you be able to perform these skills *simultaneously* at the highest level, rather than to excel at any one in particular.

Skating and Shooting

Imagine the last seconds of a breakaway—player against goalie with no one in between. How many times do you see the skater stop moving his feet and glide for the last 10 feet? It happens all the time in youth leagues. Similarly, many novice players plant both feet, glide, and set up their wrist shot when they are not on breakaways. Doing this just alerts everyone in the rink—including the goalie—that the player is going to shoot. It also gives defensive players time to catch up and interfere with the shot.

There is no magic technique for practicing quick shots in the midst of skating and stickhandling other than simply practicing just that: skate quickly, stickhandle quickly, and get your shot off quickly while doing the other two. You must challenge yourself at practice to do the basic drills as fast as you can. Even the best players in the world continue to work on shooting, passing, and skating drills. The misunderstanding that most novice players have is that these drills are for *learning* these skills, rather than for maintaining split-second timing or becoming even faster at combining the skills.

When a player can skate at an all-out sprint and, in one motion, take a big slap shot and put it right on net, he's ready to be considered for moving up to the elite leagues. At the top, the only way to stay ahead of the backchecking defender is to skate at an all-out sprint, and the opposing defenseman is going to allow you only a split second to wind up and take the shot. A lot of youth-league players with very hard shots are not ready to move up. As recruiters, we are looking way beyond the hard shot to putting it together with fast skating, stick-handling, and great hockey sense.

Continue to work on your wrist and slap shots long after you learn how to take them. Practice taking these shots while skating as fast as you can. Try to eliminate as much setup or glide time as you can before taking your shots. Again, there is no drill to practice this in particular—it can be practiced in all drills—but only if you challenge yourself to do the basic drills with this intensity.

Toe Drag

Practice the toe drag to improve your overall skating and stickhandling abilities. The toe drag is the ultimate bait-and-switch maneuver. As you approach a defender, push the puck in front of you, turn your stick blade forward so the toe of the blade is on the ice (heel of the blade is up), stop the puck's forward motion with the toe, quickly drag the puck back toward your body, and make the move around your opponent and his stick. This move consistently baits opposing players into lunging for the puck. It throws them off balance—even if they suspect the move is about to happen.

Situations for Using the Toe Drag

1. One-on-one against a defender who is skating backward: it will cause him to decrease backward speed or make a lateral move, and then you skate around him.
2. Close to the goal: toe-drag the puck back into your body, pull back, and shoot as the puck is coming toward you. This is often necessary to pull the puck out of traffic and get off a quick shot during scrambles near the crease.
3. Coming out of the corner: the defender doesn't know if you're going to go full speed or not, and this move will throw off his rhythm as he tries to find the correct angle and speed to use against you.

Practice. Place your gloves two feet apart on the ice and practice stickhandling the puck in a figure-eight pattern though the gloves. Use the toe of your stick blade to pull the puck toward you between the gloves and, in one motion, roll your blade flat to the ice to scoop up the puck and move it around the outside of the glove and away from you. Then pull it with the toe of the blade through the gloves from the other side.

When an elite player uses the toe drag in a game, it looks effortless. Fans attribute the ability to great hands or natural talent. The truth is that this move takes a lot of practice, no matter who you are. When you see it executed by a star player, I can guarantee that he or she worked on it for hours. The move is not for beginners and not every NCAA or NHL player is great at it, but many have mastered it. The toe drag is a dependable, very successful tool for propelling yourself into the elite levels.

Once you've gotten good at doing the figure eight through the gloves, practice the move while skating. Ultimately, you want to be able to pull it off at top speed—and the best players can. Increase your speed over a matter of weeks or months of practicing the toe drag.

Toe-Drag-and-Shoot Drill. The following drill comes from Quinnipiac practices. Place four cones several meters apart in a line along the top of the circles. Shooters line up at the blue line and skate to any one of the four cones, then toe-drag around it and release a quick shot.

Suppose you recover a rebound just in front of the opposing goalie during a scramble at the top of the crease. The goalie is down in the butterfly position, stick covering the five-hole—the only chance for you to score is up high, just under the crossbar (if he tries to get up, you go five-hole). You've got to quickly pull the puck away from the goalie and, in one motion, direct it back up and over him into the top of the net. This can only be done with the toe drag—you literally snatch the puck before he can cover it and shoot. This move is a great introduction to the next section, changing the release point of your shot.

Changing the Release Point of Your Shot

The toe drag is the most effective way to change the release point of your shot. Elite goalies are so good at playing the angles, it is almost impossible to score on a direct, clear shot once they've set. Most goals come from deflections, scrambles after rebounds, screens, passes, and changes in the shooter's release point.

Changing the release point of your shot changes the angle of your shot—you beat the goalie by causing him to adjust his set position from the original angle he lined up on to stop your shot. Once the goalie moves, a lot of opportunities open up—the five-hole, the corners, and redirections that are harder for him to save when in motion than when set.

Think of changing the release point of your shot as the same as deking the goalie on a breakaway, except you're doing it from 20 or 30 feet away. In either case, you are making him move and beating him to the net with your shot. Mario Lemieux was so good at changing the release point of his shot that he would shoot to the five-hole *that was going to open up as the goalie reacted to his change in release point.* When you're playing against the world's top goalies, this is how far you have to go to get the puck in the net.

Even outside of the NHL, you are going to face some very good goaltenders, many of whom are taught angles so well that no clear shots are going to get by them. If you want to be the one who scores when no one else is putting anything in the net, be just as crafty with changing the release point on long shots as you would with breakaways. Players spend much more time practicing their breakaway moves than changing the release point of their shots. In most games, however, you'll have many more opportunities to change the release point and shoot than to showcase your breakaway moves. It's a higher return-on-investment skill to acquire.

Another elite-level strategy is to cause rebounds with your shot that result in a much better scoring chance than you have on the original shot. This concept is very obvious in basketball: if you attempt a three-point shot when none of your teammates are under the basket, the other team is guaranteed to get the rebound if you don't score. In elite hockey, the shooter is often hoping to create a rebound scoring chance rather than to beat the goalie cleanly on the first shot. Again, the goalies are so good that scoring is not as straightforward as blast-

Jamie Holden, Quinnipiac's career leader in saves   Courtesy of QuinnipiacBobcats.com

ing a great first shot past them. Change the release point of your shot, and you cause the goalie to move. When he's moving, it's much harder for him to stop deflections and second shots off of rebounds.

Creating Rebounds

As mentioned above, good goalies are too good to beat on clear, long shots. You'll need to rely on teammates in front of the net to redirect, deflect, screen, or score on rebounds. Elite goalies train for years to control rebounds—their careers depend on it. They are going to catch high shots; redirect low shots directly into the corners, out of danger; or smother midheight shots. However, they have a much harder time controlling shots that are 6 to 12 inches above the ice. The best way to stop a shot at this height is to butterfly and hope to trap it.

Remember, rebounds are great scoring opportunities, often better than the opportunity you have on a clear 30-foot shot. Going for the top corner from 30 feet out and missing the net or creating a glove save and no rebound is not a higher percentage play than putting the puck low and hard on-net, resulting in a deflection or a rebound.

Passing

Amateur skaters may think that once players have advanced to the NCAA or the pros, they don't spend any more time on basic passing drills in their practices. While they don't spend time on *basic* passing drills, they do work very hard on elite versions of basic passing techniques. With a few years of hockey experience, most players are great at catching good forehand and backhand passes. But how often do they get a nice pass, tape to tape, in a close game? Instead, elite players master catching bad passes and creatively passing the puck in tough situations in ways that maximize the probability that their teammates will catch it.

The Saucer Pass

One of the most important passes to master in elite hockey is the saucer pass. While it is mentioned as early as peewee levels, most players don't actually master it. It's not that hard to lift the puck over a defender's stick when you pass it to a teammate. It does, however, take a lot of practice to have the puck land flat—and not bounce—just in time for your teammate to catch it. The elite players defending you are not going to give you open passing lanes for easy tape-to-tape passes. You have to pass between legs, under sticks, and over sticks that are purposely kept low to take away the easy passing lanes.

Getting a good spin on the puck is critical for making a good saucer pass. Like a flying saucer, the puck spins horizontally as it moves though the air. The rotation keeps the puck flat, which causes it to drop flat onto the ice and not bounce or wobble over a teammate's stick.

To achieve this, start with the puck on the heel of your blade. As you make the pass, roll the puck from the heel toward the toe of the blade, causing it to spin and stay flat. Follow though with a snap or chipping motion until you get the puck to fly without wobbling. You want the puck to sail over as many obstacles as necessary before your teammate catches it. Try to have it land just a few feet in front of his stick. The ultimate demonstration of passing skill is either to lead a saucer pass to a teammate moving at full speed that lands just at his stick or to float a saucer pass over a couple of defenders' sticks to a teammate who, in one motion, shoots off of your pass.

The Difference Is Speed

It is probably becoming clear that there are not many skills that average players can't do that elite players can do. Rather, elite players have mastered the nuances of the basic skills so that they are effective in the most demanding situations. For example, any player can pass to a teammate, but only elite players can do it with defenders in the way or in a manner that allows a teammate to shoot directly off of the pass. In certain situations, the differentiator is simply speed. A lot of players can do a toe drag while standing still, while the top players can do it at full speed in traffic.

With this in mind, never stop practicing passing as you advance in skill, but practice making and receiving difficult passes. The basic drill that you've done hundreds of times—find a partner and pass the puck back and forth—could be a waste of time after a point unless you challenge yourself to make and catch hard passes, passes to the skates, passes in the air, saucer passes, passes that are not tape to tape, and any other drills that quicken your reaction time. Work to develop skills for making or catching the pass that seems impossible, which sets you apart from the other players in the tryout.

Small-Space Stickhandling

The concept here is the same with passing: after a point, everybody can stickhandle the puck though open ice without losing it. Only the elite players can stickhandle at full speed through a very small space without losing the puck. Once you've mastered the basics, move on to drills that challenge your current stickhandling skills. In the NCAA, you're not going to have much time to stickhandle the puck from blue line to blue line in front of thousands of fans. If you want to have any serious time with the puck, it's going to come in tight quarters with intense challenges from opposing players moving full speed. Adapt your stickhandling drills to learn small-space, full-speed stick-handling. You rarely move very far in a straight line with the puck, though a lot of stickhandling drills practice just that. To prepare you effectively for elite hockey, stickhandling drills should emphasize short, intense bursts of speed and rapid changes of direction, and they should end with a shot or a pass.

3

Elite Goalie Skills

Today's elite goaltender must control not only the goal crease, but the area behind the net, the corners, and the entire slot. She's expected to stop hard rim-around shots (when the puck is shot along the boards behind the net, usually on a dump-in), make breakout passes, and lift the puck in hard clearing shots past the blue line.

In terms of skating, exceptional lateral agility, mobility, and explosiveness are required. His skating is almost always done in short bursts. The goalie must be the best skater in his area, which is not goal line to blue line, but includes behind the net and back, post to post, and forward and back within the crease. In other words, the goalie must be a great skater in a small space.

Thus, it's important that goalies take time to do the best skating drills for their position, which differ from the full-ice skating drills of the forwards and defensive players. Note, however, that you're not going to benefit from the drills if you don't do them with the proper form. Make sure your shoulders are square and your stick and blocker are down while moving. Through repetition, these drills can create the almost instantaneous reaction times needed for big saves. If you're not using good form, though, the repetition will reinforce bad habits that are very hard to change.

In addition, as with all drills, make sure you don't lose your focus on everything but the skating pattern of the drill. In other words, you have to practice being mentally on for every movement. Outside of the most elite leagues, many goalies probably don't realize that they have to practice and develop the ability to be mentally focused on every move they make.

Body and Stick Positioning While Moving

Before getting started, there are a few good and bad habits to be conscious of every time you move to position yourself for blocking a shot.

When moving across the crease to your stick side, lead with your stick blade on the ice, blocker down, glove ready, and shoulders square to the direction you're moving. Don't stand up tall to make the push. Arrows on the photos in photo collection 3.1 point out good stick and blocker positioning.

 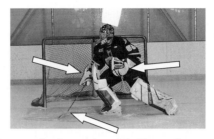 

Photo collection 3.1 Correct T-push technique, moving from right to left. The goalie starts in the set position and needs to T-push across the goal to cover the other side. The arrows point to examples of good form, including the stick blade, which remains in constant contact with the ice, and the goalie's hands, which are kept out in front of the body to better challenge shots.

In photo collection 3.2, the arrows point to several common mistakes when moving post to post. The stick is up and off the ice, and the blocker is up and to the side. In addition, the goalie is standing up, lifting up his shoulders and glove. Notice how the five-hole is wide open in the middle photo as he moves from post to post.

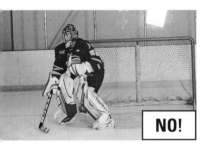 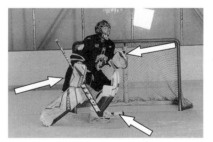 

Photo collection 3.2 Incorrect T-push technique. Here, note how the goalie's shoulders and hands come up and his stick blade comes off the ice. At the end of the T-push he isn't fully reset and, as a result, is not ready to properly defend the goal.

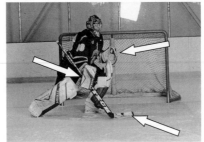

Photo collection 3.3   Correct T-push technique, moving from left to right.

Photo collection 3.3 features an example of the same glove-side post-to-post movement with good form. Notice how the stick and blocker positioning is different from photo collection 3.2. The five-hole is covered as he moves, and his shoulders and glove are not raised.

Drills for Lateral Agility and Positioning

Deflections are the big five-hole goals, not direct shots. Shooters may not admit this, but a lot of goals go in off of redirections rather than because of the shooter's ability to aim for the space that is going to be created between the goalie's legs when he moves. Knowing this, goalies have to control the openings that are created by their movements, which is a much different concept than making saves or blocking shots. The best way to work on this skill is through regular repetition of drills practicing quick movements with the right form.

The following simple, but extremely effective, small-space skating drills for goalies were developed with the help of Brian Daccord. All Quinnipiac goalies practice several variations of these drills daily.

Four Pucks in a Box

In the first series, four pucks are set up in a box that is slightly larger than the width of the net. The goalie practices moving between each set of pucks (photo collection 3.4).

The goalie should complete the entire drill within the box, moving first in one direction for one complete circle, then moving in the other direction for one complete circle.

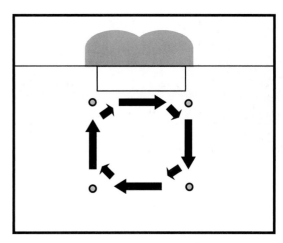

This is the how the pucks should be set up for the Four Pucks in a Box drill.

Photo collection 3.4 The goalie pivots, opens, and pushes as he squares his way between the four pucks in the box. Note how the stick blade stays in contact with the ice to protect the five-hole.

Photo 3.5   **Photo 3.6**   **Photo 3.7**

Photo 3.8   **Photo 3.9**

Photos 3.5–3.9 This shows close-ups of the Four Pucks in a Box drill. Photos 3.6 and 3.9 perfectly illustrate the T-push. Again, the stick blade remains in contact with the ice at all times.

Note the goalie's good form in photos 3.5 to 3.9. Not only is he practicing the footwork, but he leads with his stick down, shoulders square, and blocker down.

Butterfly

In this series, the goalie practices moving clockwise around the box while making butterfly saves between each set of pucks (photos 3.10 to 3.17). The goalie should use only one T-push to move between each set of pucks and make sure to move around the box in both directions, keeping proper upper-body form the entire time.

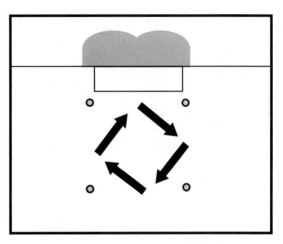

This is the puck setup and skating pattern for the Butterfly drill.

Photo 3.10

Photo 3.11

Photos 3.10–3.11   Correct technique for the Butterfly series includes emphasis on proper pad positioning (illustrated in photo 3.10, where the two pads are shown touching each other).

Photo 3.12

Photo 3.13

Photos 3.12–3.13   Using the stick blade—which is in constant contact with the ice—to protect the open five-hole when the two pads do need to be separated (as seen in photo 3.13).

Photo 3.14

Photo 3.15

Photos 3.14–3.15 A weight transfer for movement that keeps the extended pad flush with the ice while pushing off the back leg (shown in photo 3.14) such that the momentum of the push will carry the goalie through the pivot and into a ready position.

Photo 3.16

Photo 3.17

Photos 3.16–3.17 The goalie makes a full revolution around the box, moving clockwise by planting and pushing off the left skate and making sure that the stick blade, right pad, and right knee are always flush to the ice. Once complete, the player will then move counterclockwise by pushing off with his right foot (shown in photo 3.17).

Additional Drills

The drills in this section are designed to condition you to quickly position your skate for a fast butterfly-to-butterfly save.

1. Photos 3.18 to 3.23 show a drill used to practice proper technique when using the butterfly push. This is an excellent drill to practice a goaltender's edges (on his skates).

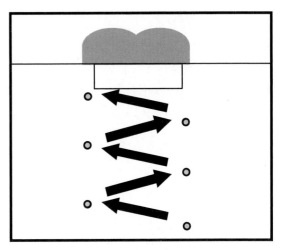

Set up six to eight pucks in alternating lines slightly wider than the net.

Photo 3.18 Stand square, facing the shooter off of the left post.

Photo 3.19 Turn your shoulders to face the far post, push hard, lead with your stick, and keep your blocker down.

Photo 3.20 Butterfly at your right post.

Photo 3.21 **Photo 3.22** **Photo 3.23**

Photos 3.21–3.23 Get up quickly, square to the shooter on your left, and then turn and repeat the sequence, moving across the net to the far post.

2. In this drill, the goalie never fully stands up and squares to the shooter. Instead, he pushes backward to the far post with his leading leg down, in the butterfly position (photos 3.24 to 3.29). The purpose of this drill is to promote good muscle memory for quick butterfly movement in a game setting. Remember to always protect the five-hole with the blade of your stick.

Photo 3.24 **Photo 3.25** **Photo 3.26**

Photo 3.27 **Photo 3.28** **Photo 3.29**

Photos 3.24–3.29 In this series, the goalie pushes his way between the pucks, working backward toward the goal. His left pad and knee remain flush with the ice while his stick blade protects the five-hole, and he moves by pushing off his left skate (illustrated in photo 3.25), keeping his right knee and pad flush to the ice. Again, note how his hands are kept properly out away from the body to cut the shooter's angle and better challenge the shot.

3. This drill works on one of the most important concepts in modern goaltender positioning. When the goalie is down from making a save, he should pick up only the leg opposite the direction he needs to move so he can immediately push to the next position in the butterfly position for the save. Photos 3.30 to 3.33 show this sequence in action.

Imagine trying to make this save if, in photo 3.31, the goalie got up with his right leg (closest to the shooter) first or tried to stand up and square himself to the shooter. At the elite levels, the speed of the game is too fast to stop this shot if you don't develop the ability to go directly from butterfly to butterfly. Many young—and old—goalies have never conditioned them-

Photo 3.30 Butterfly save, rebound bounces to . . .

Photo 3.31 . . . the goalie's right. Left leg up . . .

Photo 3.32 . . . hard push to the right . . .

Photo 3.33 . . . and immediately into butterfly position (without standing up) for the next save.

selves to push immediately into the next butterfly save with the leg opposite the shooter; instead, they get the same leg up each time, regardless of which side they have to push to for the next save.

Saving Drill

Coaches and players tend to think of shooting drills, but rarely does anyone mention a saving drill. Goalies need to ask for saving drills, which, incidentally, are also great shooting drills, so everyone on the ice benefits from the drill. With a little customization, many shooting drills can also become great saving drills that benefit both the shooter and the goalie. The next drill is a great one for working on a shooter's reaction time and accuracy *and* on the goalie's butterfly-to-butterfly move.

The following drill is designed to reinforce the *find it, see it, stop it* pattern after a rebound and the butterfly-to-butterfly second save. Goalies should train to quickly find the rebound—is it on the left, right, or center—rather than reflect on the great save he just made. Then, he must see it—the goalie has to have a visual on the puck to move to the right position to stop it.

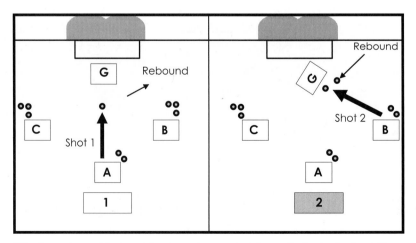

This shows the positioning of the three shooters and the goalie for the Saving drill.

Photo 3.34

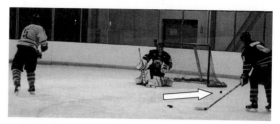

Photo 3.35

Photo 3.36

Photos 3.34–3.37 After the first save, the goalie will butterfly push in the direction of the rebound, keeping his pads touching, stick blade covering the five-hole, and hands out, ready to receive the second shot. This drill is great for muscle memory.

Photo 3.37

1. First, make a butterfly save on the first shot from Player A (photo 3.34).
2. Then, without fully standing up, push with the leg opposite the direction you need to move while keeping the other leg on the ice in the butterfly position (photo 3.35). Player B or C shoots only if the rebound bounces to his side. Player B or C should wait a half second after the initial save to take his shot (photos 3.36 and 3.37).

Stopping a Rim-Around

Effectively stopping a rim-around requires a lot of practice. Most goalies have seen the play at college or pro games. They then imitate what they saw the elite goalie doing, basically just moving behind the net, although they didn't catch all of the technique. But there is more involved than just skating behind the net to reach the puck to stop rim-arounds.

In photos 3.38 and 3.39, the goalie has skated behind the net to intercept the rim-around. On a hard shot, however, he would not be set up to effectively handle the puck; in fact, he would likely redirect it to the front of his net.

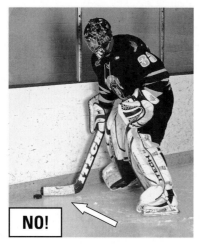

Photo 3.38

Photo 3.39

Photos 3.38–3.39 In attempting to stop the rim-around, the goalie's stick blade is incorrectly angled (3.38). The arrow in 3.39 illustrates how this leads to the puck bouncing off and toward the net as a result.

In photo 3.40, the goalie is in the right position to stop the rim-around and to prevent it from bouncing out of his control. His left skate is angled to block the puck if it skips off of his stick, and he creates a "pocket" to catch the puck between his stick and the boards.

Photo 3.40 Correct technique for intercepting the rim-around. Note the position of the stick blade in relation to the boards as compared to the previous example—this ensures that the puck is kept under control.

Photo 3.41

Photo 3.42

Photos 3.41–3.42 Both photos illustrate the incorrect technique for stopping a rim-around, here from the opposite direction.

Practice intercepting the rim-around by first setting up behind the net while your coach or teammate fires the puck around the boards. After you develop your form, switch to practicing moving from the front of the net and back to the boards to stop the puck. Make sure to practice stopping the rim-around from both directions.

In photos 3.41 and 3.42, notice how the goalie does not create a pocket between his stick and the boards. The lack of a pocket makes the puck hard to control and usually winds up redirecting it in front of the net. In addition, his legs are open and his skate is not angled to stop the puck if it does jump off of his stick.

In photo 3.43, the goalie's stick is positioned to create the pocket that traps the puck. His left leg pad is firmly against the boards to back up his stick and to catch any deflections off of his stick or high rim-around shots. His right skate is positioned to catch any deflections off of his stick that are headed between his legs or toward the net.

Photo 3.43 The correct technique for stopping a rim-around, shown here from the opposite direction.

Stickhandling, Passing, and Shooting with the Goalie Stick

Elite teams look for goalies who can contribute to the entire team effort, not just block shots. Work on your shots, passes, and stickhandling so that you can clear pucks, make breakout passes, and handle the puck in a variety of situations.

The first pass in the breakout is the most important. If it's not accurate, the breakout breaks down immediately. On dump-and-change plays and power plays, the goaltender frequently has the chance to make the first breakout pass and give his team an offensive advantage with a quick transition up ice. It is also a great advantage to have a goalie who can make long clearing shots—in the air—when necessary. Goalies have developed two different hand positions for shooting or passing: glove-over-the-front or glove-behind-the-stick. Try both and decide which you like better. Keep practicing until you can comfortably shoot the puck past the blue line in the air.

Practice using a hard wrist shot to clear the puck. The form for the goalie's wrist shot is exactly the same as a forward's, except the lower-hand (glove-hand) positioning. In photos 3.44 to 3.46, the goalie is using the glove-over-the-front of the stick hand positioning, which gives a "pulling" effect with the glove hand.

Photo 3.44   **Photo 3.45**   **Photo 3.46**

Photos 3.44–3.46   The glove-over-the-front (palm-down) stick hand positioning.

Photo 3.47   **Photo 3.48**

Photos 3.47–3.48   The glove-behind-the-stick (palm-up) hand positioning.

In photos 3.47 and 3.48, the goalie is using the glove-behind-the-stick lower-hand positioning, which gives a "pushing" effect with the glove hand.

4

Game Skills

"The average hockey fan can watch an NCAA or NHL game and figure out who the fastest skaters are, who scores the goals, who hits the hardest, and who makes the biggest saves. These are obvious aspects of hockey that often get all the glory and attention when teams win games. But there are a lot of 'little' things that go on in a game that have a direct impact on the outcome, which most people never notice.

"In truth, things like gap control, angling, blocking passing lanes, and blocking shots are not 'little' things at all. They are major points of emphasis for coaches at higher levels of hockey, and they are practiced almost every day. Doing any one of these things well, at any one point in a game, could be the difference in the outcome. In addition, teaching these concepts repeatedly so that they become part of a team's culture and identity can lead directly to a successful season.

"It is sometimes hard for young players to grasp the importance of having their stick in the right position in every situation. But ask a goalie who just faced 50 shots in a game if he would have appreciated his defensemen playing stick on puck all night and knocking 20 shots off of his total. Using your stick correctly is not a hard thing to do, but it has to be taught and become habit to be repeatedly effective.

"Another important 'little' thing is shot blocking. I always think of guys that consistently manage to not block shots in one of two ways. Either they don't care enough about the team to pay the price, or they are afraid of getting hit with the puck. Either way, this is unacceptable on a winning team. The truth is that bruises heal but losses are forever. Players and coaches all appreciate a good shot blocker, and goalies love them.

"Wayne Halliwell, who works for Hockey Canada as a sports psychologist as well as NHL, junior, and college teams, talks of the concept of 'making the unnoticed, noticed.' Coaches can make these concepts part of the culture of the team and an everyday expectation for every player. This can be done by creating awards or giving recognition to players who continually do the 'little' things well.

"The beauty of teaching these finer points is that it makes your larger, systemic concepts more successful. For example, teaching proper angling technique will make your forechecks, in both the offensive zone and the neutral zone, more effective by taking away time and space from your opponent. Teaching gap control will eliminate time spent in your D-zone and help your team's transition game.

"Today's video technology makes teaching players new concepts much easier. It is not hard to tape an NHL game, break it down into the concepts you want to teach, and put it onto a DVD to show your team. Doing this creates visualization, which is a huge component in teaching young players new things. You can then show them video of themselves after ensuing competitions for reinforcement. Then they can see for themselves the similarities or differences.

"Of course, all of this is cumulative and takes time to incorporate. But a coach often has to look beyond the next game and see the big picture in terms of winning championships and developing players. In that sense, all of these 'little' things go a long way."

—Bill Riga

Controlling the Gap

Controlling the gap between yourself and the opposing puck-carrier is the key to playing defense well. As players advance, highly skilled offensive players can effectively exploit the gap in several situations, while a weaker defensive player will be ineffective. In novice leagues, ultimately it doesn't matter if there is 15 feet of space between the defenseman and the forward as the forward skates across the blue line. However, when that forward has an 80-mile-per-hour shot that is accurate from the blue line, he's going to take it every time the opposing defenseman gives him the opportunity.

The first priority of the defenseman is to interfere with or prevent shots, passes, and effective positioning by an opposing forward. And the only way to interfere with a shot is to make contact with the opposing player's stick with your stick or your body. The first rule in gap control is to always stay within one stick-length of the opponent. You can then react quickly and interfere with his shot as he is attempting to take it. Playing a close gap against a forward who does not have the puck is also highly effective, as it eliminates him as an open passing option for a teammate. Additionally, if you stay close, you can block his rebound attempts.

As a defenseman, you need to control the gap to prevent your opponent from gaining a positional advantage, or angle, as he approaches the net. If you maintain a distance of one stick-length between yourself and the opponent, you will be skating backward, stride for stride, at the same speed as your opponent. Once your speeds are matched, it is much harder for him to make an effective move around you. If the gap is too wide, however, you will have to reduce your speed to close the gap as you and your opponent move toward the net. As you reduce your speed, the forward will have a great opportunity to accelerate past you on either side.

Angling

In addition to maintaining the proper gap between himself and his opponent, a defenseman has to play the correct angle. If you think of a pool table, imagine trying to put the ball into a pocket when there is no clear path for your shot. Then imagine that one of the balls that was previously blocking your path has moved three inches to one side. It's a tight fit, but you now have a straight shot to the pocket. The defensive player must act as the pool ball that is standing in the way of the straight path to the pocket, except that on the rink, he is blocking the straight path of both the puck and his opponent to the net behind him. The challenge is to play the correct angle. The forward can see where he is skating, while the defenseman has his back to the target. If the defenseman is slightly off, like the pool ball that was moved a mere three inches, it gives his opponent a clear path to the net.

One of the best rules for playing the correct angle is to line up your outside shoulder with the forward's inside shoulder. As long as you always keep his inside shoulder in line with your outside shoulder, he will never have a clear path to the net behind you.

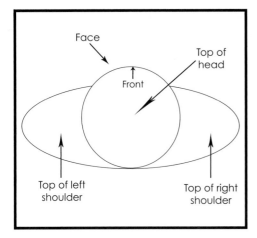

Body positioning view from above

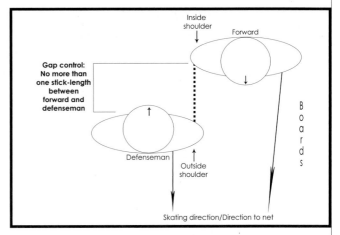

Correct positioning for defenseman: Defenseman should line up his outside shoulder with the forward's inside shoulder. This will always keep the defenseman between the forward and the net.

Closing the Gap with the Proper Angle

At some point, you have to close the gap between yourself and your opponent; otherwise, you will end up skating right into your own goalie. As you back in closer to the net, start closing the gap as you cross the blue line. By the top of the circles, you should have eliminated most of the gap and be in close contact with the forward. If you wait any longer, you'll end up backing into the goalie. From the point the forward reaches the top of the circles, he should practically have to push *through* you to advance any closer to your net.

In addition to the back-and-forth distance between the forward and the defenseman, there is a lateral distance, or side-to-side distance, that results in an angle of attack. Imagine a clock painted on the ice. The defenseman is skating backward from 12 o'clock to 6 o'clock, and the forward is skating forward in the same direction. The net is somewhere in the distance behind 7 o'clock. The defenseman should always keep his outside shoulder lined up with the attacking forward's inside shoulder. In this situation, when the forward is at 2 o'clock, the defenseman will be positioned right in the center of the clock— his outside shoulder lined up with the forward's inside shoulder and directly in his straight-line path to the net.

If the defenseman is at the center of the clock when the forward is at the 12 o'clock or 1 o'clock positions, the forward actually has a clear path to shoot or skate to the net, which is behind 7 o'clock. Likewise, when the forward makes it to 3 o'clock and the defenseman is at the center of the clock, he again has a clear shot or path to the net at 7 o'clock. These are the two most common positional mistakes a defenseman makes: he is in position to block the forward's direct forward motion but not the angle of his direct path to the net.

The right time to close the gap is when the attacking forward is at the 2 o'clock position. If the defenseman closes both the straight-

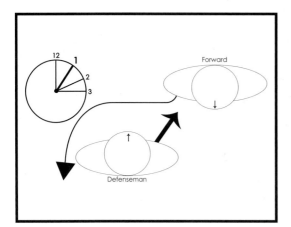

If the defenseman moves laterally to check the forward when he is in the 1 o'clock position, the forward can cut back to the center around the defenseman. In other words, the defenseman commits too early, giving the forward a chance to beat him toward the center.

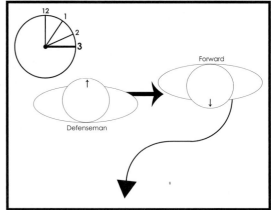

If the defenseman moves laterally to check the forward when he is in the 3 o'clock position, the forward can accelerate around the outside, past the defenseman. In other words, the defenseman commits too late, giving the forward a chance to beat him toward the outside.

ahead and the lateral gap distances when the forward is at 1 o'clock, the attacker will cut inside of the defenseman and gain the positional advantage in the center of the ice. Similarly, if the defenseman waits too long to close the gap or make the check, and the forward is at the 3 o'clock position, he is likely to make it around the outside of the defenseman as he moves toward the net.

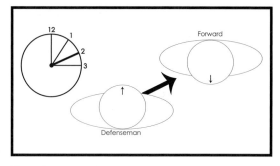

The defenseman should close both the lateral and vertical gaps when the opposing forward is in the 2 o'clock position. At this point, the defenseman is on the correct angle to prevent the forward from cutting back toward the center around him or from squeezing past on the outside.

Blocking Passing Lanes

The following techniques on blocking passes or shots are not a substitute for gap control. A good gap is the foundation upon which all good defensive moves are built (after skating skills, of course). Gap control alone can take away the bulk of an attacker's options, especially at elite levels where everything is based on split-second timing. The correct positioning of a defender's stick blade is also one of the fundamentals. The blade should always be on the ice, ideally blade-to-blade as much as possible against the attacker's stick. The defender's stick should be active: when a player's stick is passive, meaning stationary, then it is predictable and offensive players can pass around, under, or over that stick. Using an active stick is a great way to create doubt about the best passing option.

Depending on whether an opposing player is left-handed or right-handed, an elite defender will know which way he is likely to shoot or pass and will make adjustments to how he defends against each type of player. For example, a right-handed shooter skating along the left wall is likely to want to pull up and go to his forehand to pass, while a left-handed shooter in the same situation will shift into high gear and pass from his forehand side as he skates. (Note to forwards: having a great backhand pass will throw off defensemen, because they are anticipating a forehand pass in this situation.) These two resulting passing lanes will vary greatly, perhaps by as much as 15 feet, and defenders must anticipate the pass—and the passing lane—to make the slight adjustments necessary in positioning to defend against right- or left-handed shooters.

Once the action has moved to the defensive zone, dropping to one knee and extending the stick shaft onto the ice to block the passing lane with both body and stick can be effective. However, this technique must be practiced extensively so that the defender will not risk losing his balance and giving up an even better opportunity than the one he was trying to block. Don't try this move in a game until you've practiced it enough to drop, block, and get back up in a split second without losing your balance.

In short-handed situations, you have even more space to cover when blocking passing lanes. If the puck-carrier is moving laterally across the ice (not forward toward your net), he is likely trying to open up a passing lane on the side he is skating away from (by dragging you with him). You can't stay back to cover the pass because he will then be able to advance toward your net. In this situation, move laterally across the ice with him and drag your leg on the ice behind you to block his back passing lane while using your stick against his forward passing lane. Again, this takes a lot of practice to pull off in a game, but it's highly effective at countering the intended effect of opening up passing lanes on the power play.

Video is one advantage of college hockey over younger teams, and it is a great teaching tool. In slow motion, a player can see the passing lanes and where his stick should be. At full speed with adrenaline pumping, defenders don't always think of these things, and video is a very successful way to teach them. If you don't have easy access to video, watch a tape or DVD (something you can rewind and play in slow motion) of a college or NHL game. Watch the action in a different way, however, by focusing on the defenseman's positioning or what the players without the puck are doing.

Even more important at the elite levels, defenders must know if the player receiving the pass is in position to take a onetime shot off of the pass (based on whether he shoots right or left). If the receiver is in this position, he is far more dangerous to the goalie than a receiver who must stop the pass before shooting. These are the nuances that separate the elite from the rest—the receiver positions for a onetime shot, and the passer delivers the pass for the onetime shot. Anything else and the elite goalie will be set and waiting. This is especially important during a power play. Many teams set up their entire power play for onetime shots, as this prevents the goalie from setting up for saves and controlling rebounds. As you know from Chapter 3, it's hardest to make saves while in motion.

As a result of the focus on onetime shots, gap control is as important for a defender playing against an attacker without the puck as it is in defending against the puck-carrier. A good gap against an open skater will eliminate his onetime shot or passing opportunity. In two-on-two and three-on-three situations, controlling the gap against open forwards is the key to defense.

Defending a Two-on-One or Three-on-One

In two-on-one and three-on-one situations, the defender must adjust his gap accordingly. With no defensive partners to cover open attackers, the lone defender is playing a mix of gaps—those of the puck-carrier and those of the other attackers. If the puck-carrier moves laterally toward the perimeter, the outnumbered defender can extend the gap on the puck-carrier to remain in position to block some of the passing lanes, especially onetime shot options, while allowing (to some extent) wide-angle shots from the perimeter, which are much higher percentage saves for the goaltender than onetime or better angle shots.

When you're outnumbered, timing is the key to good defense. In theory, a defender's teammates are racing in as backcheckers to help. If he can throw off the attackers' timing by taking away the good passing and shooting opportunities and by forcing the offense to take time looking for higher percentage scoring chances (or letting the puck-carrier skate wide to the perimeter), the backcheckers can skate into position to cover open attackers and clear rebounds.

Constant evaluation of which attacker is in the most danger-ous position and split-second decision making are required by the defender in two-on-one and three-on-one situations. As the attackers advance further into the zone, the designation "most dangerous" will shift back and forth from the open attacker to the puck-carrier as each one moves in and out of higher percentage scoring areas. When the open attacker is setting up for a onetime shot, position yourself more in favor of disrupting that pass and let your goalie set up on the wide puck-carrier in case of a shot.

Shot Blocking

The game of hockey has changed dramatically in the past 15 years because of improved methods for blocking shots and because of the commitment of coaches and players to blocking shots, not to men-tion the effect of better equipment. In the NHL, shot blocking has been perfected to the point where it has become difficult to even get shots on net in many situations. During their run of Stanley Cups, for example, the New Jersey Devils regularly held opponents to 20 shots or less per game.

Players and coaches are moving away from the feet-first dive because opposing players are quick enough to fake a shot and slip around a diving defender. At Quinnipiac, players are taught to block shots by dropping to one knee with their down leg extended east-west to cover the greatest area while simultaneously extending their stick shaft east-west for additional coverage. In this position, a defender can cover 6 feet or more of shooting space. The closer you are to the shooter, the less room the puck has to elevate over your stick or leg. Use the goaltender's strategy of challenging the shooter: playing a close gap cuts down the shooter's angle, making it is less likely that any shot will get past you.

Defending a One-on-One in the Neutral Zone

As the attacker speeds through the neutral zone during a full-ice one-on-one, the defender should keep the attacker to his outside shoulder while he forces the attacker to the outside, away from the center of the ice. Shots become less dangerous as the angle of the shot grows wider. Of course, maintaining a good gap reduces shooting opportunities, but if a shot is taken, it's least effective from the wider angles.

In addition to gap control and lining up the forward on his outside shoulder, it is absolutely necessary for the defender to keep his stick blade on the ice. The attacker is worried about maintaining puck possession first and taking a shot second, so he can be effectively steered to the outside by the defender's stick. The defenseman should also keep his stick centered on his body and extended, while maintaining a comfortable posture.

If the defenseman maintains proper positioning against the attacker, the gap and timing become all-important; if the gap and timing are good, the defenseman can dictate how the play unfolds. As an added threat, the defenseman's extended stick is a continuous threat of a poke check and is effective in taking away much of the forward's stickhandling space and options. However, it is critical that defensemen *do not lunge forward with the poke check*! This is the biggest—and most dangerous—mistake of defensemen in the one-on-one situation, as lunging throws you off balance. Poke check as you are skating backward, and don't rely on any forward body-motion to help with your poke check or you will lose backward speed. Don't fall back on the poke check as your number one option as a defender.

In conclusion, gap control is very important. Timing is very important. If both are good, the defender can dictate the play. Defending a one-on-one well is very easy to improve; regular practice lets the defender work on his timing, and several Quinnipiac forwards have converted to defense. The learning curve is very fast, and, even at the Division I level, it's amazing how much better the new defensemen become with continuous practice. As a result, I try to run one-on-ones at least once a week in practice: if you get beat in a game it's a breakaway and maybe a goal.

Defending a One-on-One in Tight Spaces and the Corner

Stick blade versus stick blade (or puck) is a very important tool for defenders. Just as an attacking forward is looking to create time and space, the defender is there to deny it, rush it, or slow it down enough for a teammate to jump in. In small spaces such as the corner, the defender should be tight on the attacker with his stick blade on the puck at all times. The best way to stop a dynamic player is to deny him time and space to work or to deny him control of the puck. Controlled aggressiveness is key, and the best defenders are ultra-aggressive. However, they don't haphazardly chase their opponent; they are in full control and can react to anything.

One-on-One Offense

As a attacking forward, keep it simple and focus on breaking down the three fundamentals of your opponent's defense: gap control, timing, and balance. An attacking forward must create both time and space. Great forwards will change gears and the attack angle to force a bad gap and to throw off the defender's timing. This is what Gretzky was best at—creating time and space the way no other forward had previously done. His lateral cuts along the blue line or 360s at the top of the circles caused huge gaps for even the NHL's best defensemen and threw off the expected rhythm of the game so dramatically that even his own teammates were sometimes surprised to find his passes landing on their sticks.

You will have almost no success in a one-on-one if you skate straight at an elite defender and rely on fancy stickhandling to dribble the puck between his legs. In this situation, his balance, gap, and timing are all unaffected, and he will have no trouble defending against this type of play.

Instead, attack the defender's balance by showing the puck and baiting him into lunging for it, then toe drag around him. Fake a shot to stand up the defender for a split second and then explode by him in high gear as he shifts his balance to block the shot. Double pump or hesitate on a shot so you can put it between his legs or under his stick as he transitions back from what he thought was a fake shot.

5

Team Systems
and Strategies

Individual skill sets obviously play a significant role in the makeup of a team at any level. However, each player's ability to execute within a team's systems nearly always creates the difference between a successful or an unsuccessful outcome.

Systems are an important team concept that can be implemented at the earliest stages. As players advance within the sport, it is essential for each to master a strong knowledge of the team's systems for the team to excel as a whole.

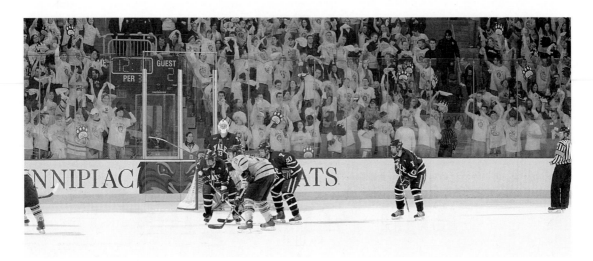

Sold out TD Banknorth Sports Center, Quinnipiac University   Courtesy of QuinnipiacBobcats.com

This chapter will cover a variety of systems that can be used. We will start with options pertaining to play in the three zones. Then we will discuss some of the possibilities for power-play and penalty-killing opportunities.

It is important for coaches to remember that the particular systems that they employ often depend on the individual skill sets of the players on their team. Whenever possible, evaluating the strengths and weaknesses of the players prior to the start of a season can assist with incorporating a basic set of systems. Whether you are a youth coach or a college coach, there are a variety of strategies that you can employ, regardless of the situation at hand. Some of these strategies will be used more extensively, while others may be reserved only for specific scenarios.

Forechecking

There are two basic types of forechecks that we will cover in this chapter, the 1-2-2 and the 2-3.

The 1-2-2

The 1-2-2 is an elementary system that is more widely used than the 2-3. In comparison to the 2-3, the 1-2-2 is easier for players to grasp. With the 1-2-2, players pursuing the puck can survey the play and disrupt the opposition.

1-2-2 Forecheck
- F1 attacks the puck.
- F2 or F3 will seal the strong-side wall and then go and help F1.
- F2 or F3 on the weak side will slide to the middle of the ice (slot area) and present himself as a shooter, or he can backcheck if the puck is turned over.
- Defensemen will adjust to the puck. Strong-side D will go to the wall and weak-side D will go to the middle of the ice. Both defensemen should be just inside the blue line.

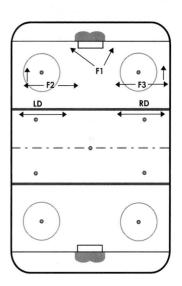

Forward Responsibilities. In the 1-2-2, the first forward (F1) aggressively pursues the puck deep into the offensive zone. If checking is allowed at your level of play, then it is imperative that F1 makes contact with the opponent.

The second forward (F2) provides support to F1 inside of the offensive zone just above the face-off circle. F2 needs to read the play and has several responsibilities. If the opposition attempts a strong-side breakout pass, then F2 needs to seal the strong side and break up the pass along the boards. The second option is for F2 to pursue the puck if an opposing player makes his way past F1. Lastly, if there is a loose puck in the offensive zone, F2 needs to alertly jump into the play in pursuit of the puck.

The third forward is stationed even with F2 but is positioned in the high slot area. F3 serves as a scoring option in prime position if F1 or F2 gain control of the puck.

If the opposing team elects to make a pass between the two defensemen, it is important for F3 to jump to the weak side. In this scenario, F2 would seal off the wall, while F1 would rotate up to the high slot.

In addition, if neither F1 nor F2 gain control, F3 can serve as a backchecker as the opposition makes its way up the ice.

Defensive Responsibilities. Primary puck pursuit in the 1-2-2 lies in the hands of the forwards. However, defensemen do have certain responsibilities within this system.

As the forwards go after the puck in the offensive zone, the defensemen are stationed at the offensive zone blue line. Their main function is to provide support to the play. Defensemen should hold the blue line and not retreat into their own zone too quickly. An early retreat creates bad gap.

If the game situation warrants it, then the defensemen will often pinch in on the play. This is a personal preference that can be implemented at any time, regardless of the situation. However, if it's late in the contest and your team is trailing by a goal, I recommend having the defensemen pinch in on the play. Most teams will pinch on a weak-side wrap at the NCAA level.

1-2-2 Summary. There are a few key premises that are essential for the proper execution of a 1-2-2 forecheck. Most important, it is imperative to stress to each player that a strong knowledge of individual responsibilities translates into successful team execution.

In addition, the forwards need to be active within the system and rotate to the correct spot. Staying stagnant or being overaggressive can contribute to a breakdown in the play. While maintaining a rotation is an issue at all levels, it is especially evident with younger players who fail to keep a high forward (F3) within the system.

The 2-3

The second type of forecheck is the 2-3. In this scenario, two players pursue the puck in the offensive zone, while the remaining three players are back at the second level. We will discuss two variations of the 2-3 in this section.

In general, the 2-3 is a forecheck that encompasses a risk-reward element. It is more complex and riskier than the 1-2-2. However, when done correctly, the reward can be greater and result in more scoring opportunities.

On the flip side, when the 2-3 is done poorly, the result is often odd-man offensive rushes for your opponent.

2-3 Forecheck

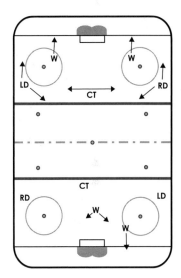

- Wings attack the puck, eliminate a defenseman-to-defenseman pass, and then help each other. When the puck moves to the half wall, one wing will help to battle for the puck and the other wing will rotate into the slot area (to be a shooter and a backchecker).
- LD and RD prepinch and hold the wall when the puck is on their side of the ice.
- LD and RD must back off to the blue line when the puck is in the opposite corner.
- CT moves along the blue line and has wall coverage on the strong side.
- Wings can also attack one hard and one soft (see the bottom half of the diagram), and the second wing reads and reacts.

Note: In order for this drill to be effective, the center must think like a third defenseman and commit to the system.

The Traditional 2-3. The basic premise of this system is that two wings aggressively attack into the offensive zone. Both players work in tandem to chase the puck. It is important to note that in this first scenario of the 2-3, the two wings are the ones highlighted, not just two of three forwards, because the center stays back with the defensemen.

In the second level, the two defensemen will flank the center at the offensive zone blue line. Once again, positioning and knowledge of responsibilities are important in this system.

If the opposition attempts to come up the wall, then the strong-side defenseman will pinch and seal off the play. In turn, the center and the weak-side defenseman will rotate into the appropriate position.

Spacing is also important in the event of a turnover on the play. In this situation, the center remains in the high slot and becomes a primary scoring option.

LW Lock/2-3 Forecheck

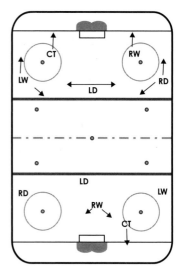

- CT and RW attack the puck, eliminate a defenseman-to-defenseman pass, and then help each other. When the puck moves to the half wall, CT or RW will help to battle for the puck and the other will rotate into the slot area (to be a shooter and a backchecker).
- LW and RD prepinch and hold the wall when the puck is on their side of the ice.
- LW and RD must back off to the blue line when the puck is in the opposite corner.
- LD moves along the blue line and has wall coverage on the strong side.
- CT or RW can also attack one hard and one soft (see the bottom half of the diagram) and the other player reads and reacts.

Note: In order for this drill to be effective, the left wing must think like a third defenseman and commit to the system.

The 2-3 Left-Wing Lock. The 2-3 is also called the left-wing lock. This name has emerged through the years, gaining notoriety by the implementation of this particular strategy by the Detroit Red Wings.

The left-wing lock holds many of the same premises as the traditional 2-3. The main differences revolve around the positioning and responsibilities of the left wing and the center.

In the traditional variation, the center sits back at the second level with the two defensemen, while the left wing pursues the puck. In the left-wing lock setup, however, the center and the right wing are the two primary forecheckers in the offensive zone.

The left wing is stationed back with the two defensemen along the left-wing wall. Otherwise, the responsibilities of each player remain similar to that of the traditional system.

Neutral Zone Play

Strong play in the neutral zone is another essential element for success. As with forechecking, there are several different options that can be used to disrupt your opponent in the neutral zone.

In this section, we will discuss two basic approaches, the F1 attack and the straight 1-2-2.

The F1 Attack

The F1 attack is a system that can be easily implemented at all levels. In fact, it is recommended for beginners and youth players due to its relative simplicity.

In this situation, the first forward (F1) who is closest to the puck (dictated by how the opposition has set up) attacks the opposition on the strong side. The other two forwards provide support. From that point, the second forward (F2) has the option of attacking with F1 or sealing the strong-side wall in an attempt to limit options for the opponent and gain control of the puck.

Meanwhile, F3 remains in the center of the ice, ready to provide support for his teammates.

Neutral Zone F1 Attack

- F1 attacks the puck.
- F2 seals the strong-side wall and then can go help F1.
- F3 stays in the middle of the ice in support.

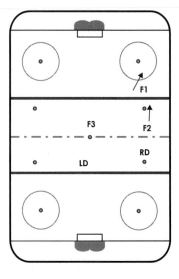

Neutral Zone 1-2-2

The neutral zone 1-2-2 is used at levels where players are slightly more advanced. One of the key factors in determining whether this system is the right one to use is to gauge if the defensive players at your level of play are making defender-to-defender passes.

If they are, then the 1-2-2 is a good route to take. If they are not, then the F1 attack might still be your best bet.

The positioning within the 1-2-2 is as follows. The center sits up high at the top of the formation near the offensive zone blue line. The two wings make up the second level of support and station themselves even with the neutral zone face-off dots just in front of the red line. Lastly, the two defensemen sit back near the defensive zone blue line on the inside of the face-off dots. All three forwards are interchangeable.

For this system to be effective, you want your center (F1, in this case) to split the ice in half and funnel toward the outside at the opposing player with the puck. Once F1 has funneled, the strong-side wing will come up into the play as the second attacker. It is also important to note that in this situation—and especially at advanced levels—F1 should employ good stick positioning to cut off the passing lanes. F1 must have good spacing with F2 and F3.

Lastly, it is the responsibility of F3 to slide to the middle of the ice to clog up any passing lanes once F1 and F2 are pursuing the puck in the neutral zone.

When the puck is moved within the neutral zone, the defensemen also have certain responsibilities. As the play shifts to the strong side, the strong-side defenseman slides over the face-off dot. This gives him the option to go back toward the middle of the ice or to pursue the puck near the wall if necessary. Meanwhile, the weak-side defenseman moves over near the center of the ice.

A good rule of thumb for defensemen to follow in this system is to remain inside the face-off dots. As a unit, the intent is to keep the puck outside by clogging up the center of the ice.

All players must think about passing lanes and have their sticks blocking those lanes.

Neutral Zone 1-2-2
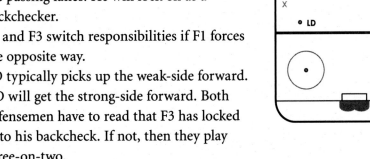

- F1 cuts the ice in half and forces the puck-carrier toward F2 or F3.
- F2 attacks the puck-carrier once he is angled into his area.
- F3 slides to the middle of the ice to clog the passing lanes. He will lock on as a backchecker.
- F2 and F3 switch responsibilities if F1 forces the opposite way.
- LD typically picks up the weak-side forward. RD will get the strong-side forward. Both defensemen have to read that F3 has locked onto his backcheck. If not, then they play three-on-two.
- LD and RD switch responsibilities if F1 forces the opposite way.

Backchecking: Defensive Zone

Keeping the puck out of your defensive zone is always the intent. When the puck ends up there, however, as it often will, you need to minimize trouble spots.

When the puck is sent into your end, the strong-side defenseman should pursue it while the other defenseman should be positioned in front of the net.

From that point, the center plays a pivotal role in dictating the play. He can immediately assist with puck pursuit or wait to see if his defenseman comes up with the puck before assisting with the breakout.

The two wings fall into place based on where the puck goes. The weak-side wing will situate himself in the high slot even with the top of the face-off circle. The strong-side wing will retreat to a position where he can successfully block a pass that is intended for an opposing defenseman.

It is also important for both wings and the weak-side defenseman to keep their sticks on the ice at all times to disrupt the passing lanes.

Defensive Zone Coverage

- D1 attacks the puck and CT supports D1 on the puck.
- D2 is in front of the net.
- RW covers the point.
- LW covers the high slot area and the point.
- If the puck switches corners, RW will move to the high slot and LW will move to cover his point, and D2 will go to the corner and D1 will go to the front of the net.

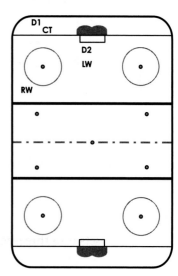

Cycling

Cycling is a system or strategy used in elite hockey that requires very strong individual skills as well as great hockey sense. The idea is to move the puck along the perimeter of the offensive zone through a rotation of players (the cycle) in an attempt to wear down the opposition's defense and create scoring opportunities.

Imagine three players in a triangle along one half of the offensive zone sideboards. The triangle rotates so that the player on the boards moves along the boards and out toward the center, while the player from the center is skating in the opposite direction and then heading toward the boards. The puck-carrier is always the player along the boards, and he protects the puck by keeping it on the outside, with his body between it and the defenseman at all times. As the puck-carrier moves along the boards, he can chip the puck off of the boards back to his teammate who is cycling into position behind him to receive the puck. Alternatively, if the cycling has been effective, the puck-carrier will spot an open lane (because the defensemen are moving around to cover the cycle) to make a centering pass or to skate the puck toward the net.

Thus, in cycling, an offensive player carries a puck along the wall, protecting the puck from the inside defenseman; a second offensive player supports underneath the puck-carrier; and the puck-carrier chips the puck along the wall to the second offensive player. The third forward, who should begin at the front of the net, can fill in to support in the same manner for the second forward once the first forward is high enough to be the backchecker. This motion is a three-person rotation that is very similar to a circle, hence the term *cycling*. The puck should always be cycled toward the boards; if it is cycled toward the middle, it defeats the purpose as it eliminates the puck protection element and can lead to turnovers. The puck is always cycled back down toward the goal line.

To practice cycling, the coach chips the puck into the corner and sets up a three-person cycle that goes for several rotations before centering the puck for a onetime shot and letting the next three skaters practice. For teams just getting started practicing the timing and spacing required to cycle effectively, all four corner face-off circles can be used by different three-person groups to practice running the cycle several times before incorporating any passes or shots.

Ultimately, the three-person cycle can involve a defenseman jumping in (via a pass back to the point rather than chipping it to the next forward).

Teams can also practice moving the cycle from one side to the other via a defense-to-defense pass. In this situation, all five skaters are involved, and a quick transition to the opposite side is required to move the cycle across the ice.

Cycling

All three forwards will cycle the puck back down the wall. It's important to keep the puck low in the offensive zone. It's also important to have at least one forward in the high slot to be a shooter and a backchecker in case of a turnover. The forwards cycle in a circular motion. F1 will skate up the wall and pass the puck back down the wall to F2. F3 will replace F2, and F1 will replace F3.

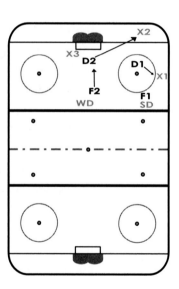

Face-Offs

Players practice positioning and systems for all situations on every part of the ice; during play, however, anything can happen—a player might fall, the puck can take a strange bounce, or there could be an unexpected transition. In these situations, which make up most of the game, players react and move according to the overall plan, but they are really relying on their hockey sense and split-second decision making at each moment. The one exception is the face-off, the only time when players know exactly where everyone is going to be at that moment and thus can have a very specific plan for what to do in the event that they win—or lose—the draw.

The most common misconception about face-offs is that they are won by just the center (or the drawman). In fact, the wings and defensemen are vital to winning face-offs at every level. Usually, there is not a clean win, and the puck will be loose in various areas around where it was dropped. The wings and defensemen must have great face-off intensity and pounce on loose pucks. As a team, a range of plans and strategies for who goes where, depending on which area the loose puck ends up in, is critical for face-off success.

Over time, it would seem that the won/lost ratio for face-offs would tend toward 50 percent. However, teams with great face-off systems regularly end up in control of the puck or the play more than half of the time. While a lot of time is probably spent on different systems for where players should line up for face-offs, not as much emphasis is placed on the more important roles of how players should play the puck or their opponent in a variety of situations immediately after the puck is dropped. All five players have responsibilities when the draw is won or lost.

The following are examples of successful face-off systems we've used recently at Quinnipiac.

Quinnipiac Face-Off Play 59

- F1 and F2 go to the net.
- D2 sets the pick.
- D1 shoots or passes.

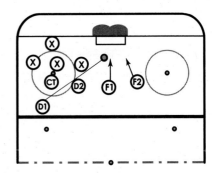

Quinnipiac Face-Off Play 59

Quinnipiac Face-Off Play 51

- CT picks.
- F1 goes to the post.
- D1 has a shot or pass.
- F2 picks.
- If we lose the draw, then CT, F1, and F2 attack the puck and D1 and D2 release back.

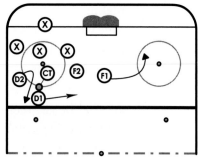

Quinnipiac Face-Off Play 51

Cashman Power-Play Face-Off

- If we lose the draw, F1 and CT attack the puck with F2 handling weak-side wrap.
- D2 goes in and releases back to cover.
- CT picks the center.
- D1 has a shot or pass.
- F1 goes in and goes to the net.
- F2 slides down and wide for a onetime shot.

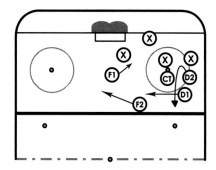

Cashman Power-Play Face-Off

Quinnipiac Face-Off Play 57

- If we lose the draw, both F1 and F2 attack the puck with one behind and one in front of the pick.
- D1 releases to stop wrap.

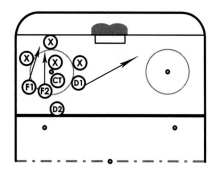

Quinnipiac Face-Off Play 57

6

Special Teams: Power Play and Penalty Kill

Special teams are an integral part of the game of hockey at all levels. Successful execution in power-play and penalty-kill situations often makes the difference between a win or loss.

A great breakout and forecheck are essential to having a good power play. Most teams make the mistake of focusing exclusively on the setup of the power play once they have control of the puck in the offensive zone. Much of their time, however, is spent recovering icings and forechecking to control dump-ins. These are the two areas in which great power-play teams really exploit their numerical advantage.

Power-Play Breakout and Forecheck

The main focus of the breakout should be to get the puck up ice with all players in position to cover all areas in case it's dumped in. It's a waste of time for one attacker to burst up ice and dump it in or take a long shot without his teammates up in position to control the loose puck. Always try to skate the puck into the offensive zone on a power play and skate it in as a unit with all attackers in place.

Most elite short-handed units are so good at killing penalties that they can often eliminate the primary objective of the power-play breakout: skating the puck into the zone. If the penalty killers clog up the defensive blue line, take what they give you and dump it in. At that point, the race is on and the team with the best training and systems execution—not to mention intensity—is going to recover the loose puck. If it's the team on the power play, they can then bring it into a controlled setup; conversely, if it's the short-handed team, they can ice the puck.

Power-Play Breakout

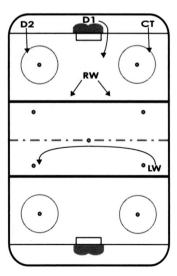

- D1 will bring the puck up the middle of the ice; the options are CT and D2.
- CT and D2 stay wide in their lanes.
- RW supports CT or D2 when the puck is passed to the outside lane.
- LW is the stretch forward. His job is to create bad gap and then get his feet moving so that he can forecheck on any dump-in.

As the power-play unit has an extra attacker or two, this is where systems execution (breakout, forecheck, and power-play setup) has the highest probability of working. At Quinnipiac, we use as many as five power-play breakouts per season. It's always good to have options, especially because opponents will try and throw you off by changing their penalty-kill forechecks.

In a variety of penalty-kill forechecks, the defenders send either one or two forwards in after the puck. The response is to position a "stretch" forward far up ice (by the far blue line) so that once the forwards get by their forecheckers, their defense will have bad gap. Similar to most youth leagues, NCAA hockey doesn't have a two-line pass rule. In leagues that don't allow the two-line pass, the stretch forward should set up closer to the red line.

Four-Wide Power-Play Breakout

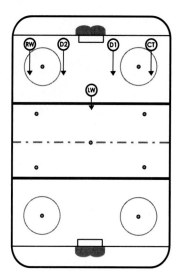

- D1 or D2 will carry the puck up the ice in his lane.
- RW and CT stay in their lanes and are support options.
- LW stays in the middle of the ice and will support RW or CT when the puck moves to either outside lane.

Note: This breakout is very effective against teams that run a 1-3 penalty-kill forecheck. When the opponent stacks the blue line, there is no need for a stretch forward.

Quinnipiac celebrates a goal versus Harvard   Courtesy of QuinnipiacBobcats.com

The stretch forward starts on the same side of the ice as the left forward in the three-wide formation. The stretch forward will skate along the far blue line to come up to full speed, then cut into the zone quickly to cover the right side on a dump-in. The left forward is responsible for the left side of the ice on a dump-in or forecheck, and the middle forward can go to either side to double-team an opposing skater who attempts to recover the dump-in.

Against a 1-3 penalty-kill forecheck (or diamond forecheck—which is very popular in the NHL and college hockey right now) a stretch forward isn't needed, as the opposing team has all of its skaters holding back. In this case, the power-play team's five skaters need to be moving up ice together with speed because, with all the defenders holding up the far blue line, they will have to dump it in. In this instance, it's good to use four wide with one forward spearheading the attack ahead of the four supporters.

The forecheck is set up at this point. The outside wide forwards attack their respective corners, and the front forward attacks the puck on the dump-in. Once the players are engaged and battling for the puck, all three forwards are put on the puck. The sole objective at this point is that they must win the puck! There is no need for one of the forwards to set up in shooting position if the power players don't yet have the puck. This is probably one of the most common mistakes in youth leagues: players on the power play set up in offensive positions before their team gains control of the puck, making it easier for the penalty killers to ice it.

Offensive Zone Power-Play Setup

The power play is a formal version of what teams should try to accomplish offensively even when no one is serving a penalty: a positional and numerical advantage that results in a good scoring opportunity. In other words, the five-on-five strategy is based on trying to create isolated three-on-two, two-on-one, or one-on-none advantages that appear and disappear at different times and places on the ice. The goal is to create the advantage and then exploit it for a goal-scoring opportunity.

The only difference on a power play is that you actually start out with the additional player from the outset. You still move the puck around in an attempt to create isolated four-on-two, three-on-one, or two-on-none situations for a great scoring chance.

For starters, it is essential to note that as a coach, the decision for what type of power play to run will be dictated by what you have for personnel. We will discuss several of those options now, starting with the overload.

The Overload Power Play

The overload is the easiest type of power play to teach and also the easiest to run as a coach and as a team. Even if your team does not have a high skill level, you can still maintain a level of effectiveness with the overload. As a result, this variation is very popular, especially with younger players.

In this scenario, the intent is to overload players on one side of the ice. Typically, one forward will be stationed below the goal line in a strong-side corner. Another forward will station himself along the half wall, while a defenseman will hold down the strong-side point. It is

Game time at the TD Banknorth Sports Center, Quinnipiac University   Courtesy of QuinnipiacBobcats.com

not necessary for the strong-side forwards to all shoot from the same side, but it is recommended. Typically, two right-handed shot (RS) forwards would be on the left side of the ice with a left-handed shot (LS) forward in front of the net, optimizing your shooting opportunities. From the right side of the ice, you would have the opposite.

The remaining forward and defenseman position themselves in the center of the ice. The forward will sit between the circles in the slot, while the defenseman will stay just inside the blue line.

The overload is especially effective when the opposition is employing a passive penalty kill with limited movement. Specifically, when the opposition is in a box setup, the intent of the overload is to create a two-on-one situation with one of the opposing players down low.

Overload Power Play

The two right-handed shot (RS) forwards will work give-and-go, and both have the option to pass to the left-handed shot (LS) forward in front of the net.

Note: This power play is very effective against teams in a passive box penalty kill. The two right-shot forwards will have a two-on-one advantage against their defenseman. This power play can also be run on the other side of the ice.

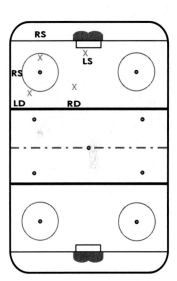

The Umbrella Power Play

The umbrella is another option that can be implemented on the power play. Simply put, this system is the coverage of the perimeter by three players.

Umbrella Power Play

The three players up top form a semicircle, or "umbrella." It is important to have a right-handed shot (RS) on the left side and a left-handed shot (LS) on the right side, as this setup presents better shooting options.

Note: This power play is very effective against a passive box penalty kill because of the multiple shooting lanes that are available.

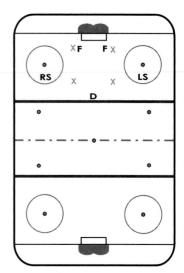

To run a successful umbrella, you have to have one true quarterback on the power play, if not two. A strong quarterback possesses the intangibles that allow him to create both time and space. In addition, your primary player along the half wall has to be poised and skilled with the puck.

In the first option of the umbrella, three players cover the perimeter, while two forwards are stationed right in front of the goalie. Traffic is the key to this setup. There is not as much of an emphasis on positioning of players based on their shot.

In the second scenario, three players form a straight line through the center of the offensive zone. A left-handed shot is set up on the perimeter just above the right circle to have a good shooting lane. A right-handed shot sets up just above the left circle to create the same effect on that side.

The third alternative bears some similarities to the perimeter positioning of the first option. In this situation, however, a left-handed shot sets up to the left of the goaltender even with or just below the goal line. Meanwhile, a right-handed shot camps right in front of the goalie to have an open shooting lane and to generate traffic. Actually, although the preference would be to have a right-handed shot in this last position, it is not necessary. It's more important to have a player with a strong shot in this spot than someone who is there only because he is a right-handed shot.

Over the years, the umbrella has become a more popular approach. In the old days, the penalty kill was often done in a box, and the umbrella gives you great shooting lanes in this scenario. For the umbrella to truly be effective, though, you must have traffic in front to screen the goaltender and generate second chances off of rebounds.

The 1-3-1 Umbrella

The 1-3-1 umbrella is a variation of the traditional umbrella noted earlier. This system is really only used at higher skill levels due to its complexity.

1-3-1 Umbrella Power Play
- The three players up top form a semicircle, or "umbrella." It is important to have a right-handed shot (RS) on the left side and a left-handed shot (LS) on the right side, as this setup presents better shooting options.
- LS2 has passing options to RS2 in the slot or RS1 off the backdoor.

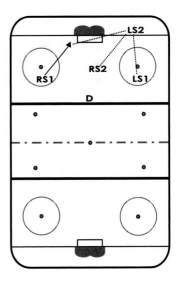

Note: This power play is very effective against a passive box penalty kill because of the multiple shooting lanes that are available.

One of the best scenarios to use the 1-3-1 umbrella is when you are going up against an aggressive penalty kill. That's because there is a dead spot in the middle that can open up the opportunity for high-quality scoring chances.

The spacing for the 1-3-1 umbrella goes as follows. Typically, two right-handed shots will set up on the left-wing side—one below the goal line and one at the half wall. Another player will station himself in front of the goalie, while a left-handed shot will set up even with RS1. The final player is at the top of the slot.

There is also an opportunity for success with this alternative because of the ability to run backdoor plays. It must be stressed again, however, that this option works best with a very high skill level. Its effectiveness will certainly be compromised at lower levels.

The High-Low Umbrella

The high-low umbrella is another option for those at higher skill levels, one that a lot of NHL teams like to use. The term *high-low* refers to the placement of the two forwards in front of the net. Basically, the system allows you to implement a double-screen in front of the goalie, which makes it extremely challenging for that netminder. One forward is stationed right in front of the net

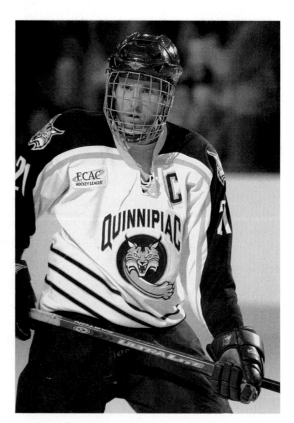

Reid Cashman, three-time All-American
Courtesy of QuinnipiacBobcats.com

(low), while the second forward is stationed in the high slot about 15 feet from the top of the crease (high).

If you have a player with a strong right-handed shot, you have the option of feeding him shots in the high slot. If you don't, then you can place two players in front to create the double-screen. The first option is the best if you have a team with an aggressive penalty kill. If the opposition has a more passive penalty kill and you have accurate shooters, then the latter might be better suited for your club.

High-Low Umbrella Power Play

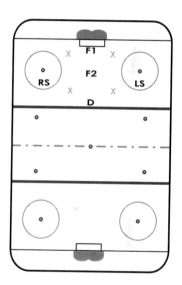

- The three players up top form a semicircle, or "umbrella." It is important to have a right-handed shot (RS) on the left side and a left-handed shot (LS) on the right side, as this setup presents better shooting options.
- F1 and F2 implement a double-screen in front of the goalie. This is extremely challenging for the goalie.

Note: This power play is very effective against a passive box penalty kill because of the multiple shooting lanes that are available.

The Box and One Power Play

The box and one is another power-play option. Like the 1-3-1 umbrella, it is an alternative that is intended for a team with a high skill level. Teams running the box and one need to be able to move the puck quickly.

Three players are set up across even with the bottom of the face-off circle. Two players then position themselves just inside the blue line. Two of the forwards line up with the two defensemen and form a box, while the fifth player is stationed in the slot.

This system allows some flexibility. Players can filter in at the top of the box based on the shot and regardless of position. The forward in the middle can shoot either way. The outside forwards in the box must be on their off wing. A right shot on the left side and a left shot on the right side allows better shooting and passing opportunities. The system should be run with an opportunity for the center forward to kick just inside the circle for a shot after a pass from outside the box.

Box and One Power Play

- Players should move the puck quickly around the perimeter of the box. The left-handed shot (LS) has options to pass to RS1 off the backdoor or RS2 in the slot.
- Another effective play is for either of the defensemen to get shots to the net. All three forwards are now in excellent position for rebounds.
- RS2 must screen the goalie when either defenseman has the puck, and then he can move to open space when the puck is passed down to LS.

Note: RS2 could also be a left-handed shot, and then the entrance pass would come from RS1.

The Penalty Kill

Playing short-handed is a part of hockey. There will always be break-downs, either physical or mental, that lead to your team playing a man down at some point in a contest.

The In-Zone Penalty Kill

In a passive penalty kill, there are two options, a box or a diamond. The box is best suited for lower levels. It's easier to teach and simpler for players to grasp at a young age. The diamond is more advanced and can be shifted into depending on the situation. Typically, the diamond will be used against an umbrella power play.

For all penalty killers, it is imperative that players remain active with their sticks and make all efforts to break up passing lanes. Players need to remain in position for the system to remain effective. Otherwise, the puck will probably end up in the back of your net.

Box Penalty Kill

- The four players on the ice form a box and try to keep the puck on the perimeter.
- The effectiveness of this penalty kill is based upon allowing only low-percentage perimeter shots.
- Both defensemen should collapse on the net to clear rebounds when a shot is taken.

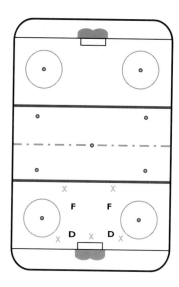

Diamond Penalty Kill

- The four players form a diamond shape.
- F1 and D1 move out and back. If the player they are defending has the puck, they extend out while the opposite side contracts back toward the net.
- D2 has net-front responsibility. Typically, he has to cover both forwards in front; therefore, he cannot lock on to just one forward.
- F2 has the responsibility of guarding the player on top of the "umbrella."

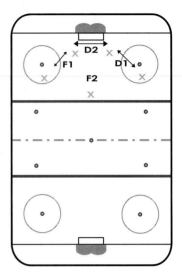

Note: This is very effective against any variation of the umbrella power play. It is very important, at higher levels of hockey, that players stay in the shooting lanes and block shots.

The Pressure Rotation Penalty Kill

The rotation, or pressure rotation, does not necessarily revolve around the premise of maintaining position, as is the case with the box and diamond. For this to be effective, players must kill the penalty as a unit of four and forget the typical forward/defenseman responsibilities. As they rotate, they will switch positions to cover the front of the net or point.

In this scenario, two forwards are lined up across just above the top of the face-off circle. The two defensemen are stationed just in front of the cage on the strong side.

It is the responsibility of the strong-side defenseman to follow the puck into the corner behind the goal line and then pursue it up the wall. Putting pressure on the opposition players and forcing them into a turnover or a bad decision is the intent. You don't want to give the opposition the chance to set up their power play. When the forward passes the puck to a teammate on the goal line, then the net-front defenseman will attack, with the weak-side forward rotating down to cover the front of the net.

Through the years, the pressure rotation has become a more popular option. In the 1970s, NHL teams were regularly connecting at a success rate of anywhere from 25 to 30 percent. However, in the 1980s, pressure rotation became more prominent—to the point where a 20 percent success rate is now considered outstanding.

Nevertheless, it is again important to note that this is an option that should be used with more highly skilled players. This strategy is not for beginners—they are better suited with learning the basics of the box or the diamond.

Pressure Rotation Penalty Kill

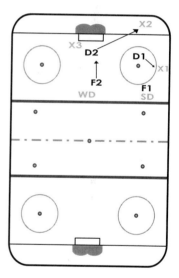

- In order for the pressure rotation penalty kill to be effective, all four players must commit to immediate and sustained pressure. The object of this penalty kill is to not allow the power play any time to set up and run plays.
- D1 attacks X1.
- F1 cuts off a pass to the strong-side defenseman (SD).
- When X1 passes to X2, D2 attacks X2.
- F2 will anticipate and rotate down to cover the front of the net.
- All four players should be aware of the passing lanes at all times and extend "stick-on-puck" (the blade of the defender's stick on the blade of the offensive player's stick).

Note: This penalty kill can be used only at elite levels. It is very high risk and high reward, but when executed effectively, it is the most successful penalty kill option. The player that is typically left open is the weak-side defenseman (WD). If the puck does somehow get to WD, then F2 will have to slide back out in a shooting lane against him and D2 and D1 will have to collapse back to the front of the net.

7

Coaching Ice Hockey

Time management, organization, and planning are critical skills needed to build the foundation of a successful hockey program. These skills are more important in coaching than the coach's playing ability or experience, which is why many professional coaches succeed even though they didn't play at the elite levels of the sport they are coaching. Professional coaches exchange ideas, new drills, teaching techniques, and practice-planning strategies at coaching seminars long after their own playing days are over. And the good news for new parent coaches is that, if you are a great teacher, open to new ideas, and a student of the game, it's not necessary to have played hockey to be a great coach.

One of my favorite parts about writing this book was the many in-depth conversations I had with hockey's leading coaches. We discussed their most recent and most profound ideas about coaching, and they contributed numerous innovative planning, teaching, and management strategies to this chapter. After discussing what is done right and what most needs to be improved in coaching youth hockey, one thing became very clear: according to all of our contributing coaches, time management needs the most improvement.

Hockey Math: Time and Resource Management

Before going into the finer points the coaches have to offer, take a look at the "hockey math" below. This math is what all great practice (and season-long scheduling) plans should be based on. Consider what happens during a game on an average team:

- Johnny plays center on his youth team, which has three lines, and plays his 15-minute periods. How much ice time does he get per game? *Answer: 3 periods × 15 minutes / 3 lines = 15 minutes of skating time*
- If Johnny is averaging one to two shots per period, how many shots will he take per game? *Answer: three to six shots per game*
- Johnny probably gets less than 1 minute of cumulative puck time—time when he's controlling the puck—per game.

In summary, one game in Johnny's youth league is worth 15 minutes of skating time, three to six shots, and 1 minute of puck time. If

Johnny has to spend 30 minutes commuting to the rink and changing before the game and another 30 minutes changing and commuting after the game, and the game lasts one hour, Johnny is (and most likely his parents are) spending two hours to skate for 15 minutes and handle the puck for about 1 minute.

Compare this to the hockey math when Johnny attends a well-organized, one-hour practice.

One-hour practice

- On ice: 60 minutes
- Shots: 40
- Puck time: 30 minutes

In the same two-hour time slot, Johnny went from skating 15 minutes to skating 60 minutes, took perhaps 10 times more shots, and got 300 percent more puck time.

If we take out the commuting time and focus on just the one hour of ice time, these are the numbers comparing the average game and the well-organized practice:

Game

- On ice: 33 percent of the time
- Shots: once every 12 minutes
- Puck time: 1 second every minute (average)

Practice

- On ice: 100 percent of the time
- Shots: once every 90 seconds
- Puck time: 30 seconds every minute (average)

Keep this math in mind when you plan your team's drills and practices. As a coach, your primary goals include maximizing skating time, puck time, and the number of shots, saves, and passes. The best way to do this with an entire team is to use drills that simultaneously incorporate skating, shooting, and puck time *and* to have as many players as possible doing the drill at the same time.

Later in this chapter, you'll find a classic warm-up drill, the Mini-Russian Circle (see page 107). In this drill, the team is divided into two lines stationed in the corners on opposite sides of the net. The first player in the first line skates out to the blue line, turns back into the zone, receives a pass from the first player in the opposite line, and then shoots. The player who made the pass then starts the process over again. Take a snapshot of this drill at any point, however, and you will see that there are 14 players standing still at all times while only 1 player is skating. If the point is to warm up the skaters and the goalie, this drill is a total waste of time.

On the other hand, imagine how much more would be accomplished with the following scenario. For the first minute, the players all line up along the side boards with pucks and skate in their own space for one minute to practice carrying the puck and turning in both directions. In the next minute, they pair up and make 20 passes.

Compare the hockey math for 2 minutes of each of these two drills:

Mini-Russian Circle
- Skating time: 2 minutes total (12 players each skating individually, with only 1 player in motion at any given time)
- Passes: 12 (1 pass every 10 seconds)
- Puck time: A fraction of the total, as players have control of the puck only momentarily before shooting

Second example
- Skating and puck time: 12 minutes (12 players were in motion for the 1 minute, and each had a puck the entire time)
- Passes: About 120 passes (1 pass every 3 seconds per pair or 6 passes every 3 seconds for the team)

Tips for Maximizing Practice Time

When you're designing a practice for an entire team, you have a responsibility to make sure you maximize skill development though the efficient use of your players' time. One tip is to save chalk talk for off-ice talks because on-ice time is too precious to use for explaining something that you can easily do before or after the practice. Communicate to your players that every practice begins with the chalk talk and practice plan 15 minutes before they step on the ice.

Another tip is to regularly evaluate your drills. If you notice that there are more players standing around in line than skating, redesign

---

Practice like You Play—Until the Whistle

"A good youth-hockey coach can become a great youth-hockey coach if he or she coaches every shooting drill until the whistle. Right now, kids are trained to tune out as soon as they shoot during drills: the shooter decreases his speed and skates back to the line, and the goalie slowly gets up after making the save and looks for the next shooter in the drill. How unrealistic is that?! In a game, immediately after the shot, the shooter charges hard into the corner or to the net for his rebound, and the goalie scrambles to find the rebound and move to block the next shot off of the rebound. Most shooting drills condition kids to do just the opposite. If coaches have the players run each round of the drill until they hear the whistle, they will become conditioned to skate hard for their rebounds and take the second shot, and goalies will develop their ability to react to the rebounds and move to block the next shot, rather than not even looking for it."

—**Brian Daccord**

the drill to accomplish the same goals with a much better use of their time. In addition to teaching the skill or strategy you want to communicate, always evaluate drills based on how efficiently they utilize time relative to skill development. Customize or adapt the standard drills to increase these key performance indicators:

- Skating time
- Puck time
- Number of shots, saves, or passes

Tournaments

Hockey tournaments are a great way to bond with teammates, play against teams outside of your area, and have a lot of fun. However, it is not uncommon for elite youth teams to compete in 10 or more tournaments per season, which elite coaches believe is not a productive allocation of time or resources.

Consider the typical three-day tournament, during which each team plays five games of 15-minute periods. On a team with three lines, each skater plays for only 75 minutes during the three days. If hotel, travel, entry fees, and other expenses total a modest $500 for the trip, that is a very expensive way for a kid to skate for 75 minutes—not to mention that a 72-hour tournament is a long time to commit to achieving just over an hour of ice time. If the player takes 15 shots during the tournament, he or she is spending over $30 per shot and is not even being offered a good opportunity to develop the core skills needed to move to the next level of play.

Hockey Camps

Compare the tournament's $500 cost, 72-hour time commitment, 75 minutes of ice time, and 15 shots to a weeklong intensive camp run by elite coaches. For approximately the same $500, the camp offers up to three hours per day of on-ice time per player plus off-ice training and the opportunity for more than 100 shots per day. The difference between the level of utilization of scarce resources—time, ice time, funds, instruction, and puck-time-per-player—is staggering.

In the first chapter, I described what attributes NCAA coaches seek in new recruits. Academic performance and well-rounded character were at the top of everyone's list. The coaches aren't all saying this because they're required to or because they want to make people feel good. The truth is, players who aren't academically qualified cause us more trouble than we have time to deal with, and those who aren't well rounded have a difficult time making the adjustment to the increased pressure of an elite athletic and academic life in college. If I could choose between attending a fourth tournament or spending those 72 hours focusing on academics, hobbies, or other sports, I'd take the latter every time. Keep in mind that the tournament really only provides just over an hour of ice time per player.

Elite Coaching at Any Level: Maximizing Puck Time

To maximize puck time, we've adapted most skill-development drills to the point where all of the players on the ice can do the drill at the same time. When players work on stickhandling, specifically the toe drag, for example, they work in small spaces. The most critical plays of the game always take place in small spaces: the corner, between the boards and a defender, in the slot, and so on. Having players work on their stickhandling, turning, and passing in small spaces develops these small-space skills much more effectively than skating through wide-open ice. The beauty of this approach is that instead of being a drawback when space gets cramped with the players all practicing on the ice together, the tight spaces provide great skill-development opportunities.

One of the ways to maximize both instruction time and puck time is to break up the skaters into small groups of five that rotate between stations, each taught by a different coach or coaches.

What follows are practice drills, broken out by age group, covering ages 6–8, 9–10, 11–12, 13–14, high school and junior hockey, and college.

Practice Drills, Ages 6–8

The following drills are appropriate for players ages 6–8.

Skating Warm-Up: Zigzag, Phase One
5 MINUTES

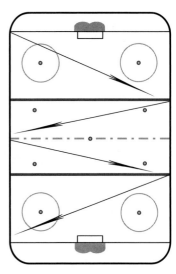

Skating Warm-Up: Zigzag, Phase One

- Player starts in the corner and skates forward to the far blue line, and then stops.
- Player proceeds to the red line and stops.
- Player then proceeds to the next blue line and stops.
- Player finishes drill by skating to the goal line and stopping.

Focus
- Long forward stride
- Two-footed hockey stops
- Quick starts

Zigzag, Phase Two

5 MINUTES

- Player starts in the corner and skates forward to the far blue line and stops.
- Player then skates backward to the red line and stops.
- Player proceeds forward to the next blue line and stops.
- Player finishes drill by skating backward to the goal line and stopping.

Focus

- Long forward stride and backward C cuts
- Two-footed hockey stops (both forward and backward)
- Quick V starts

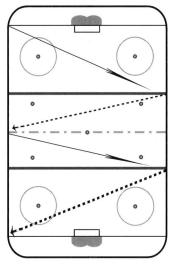

Zigzag, Phase Two

Passing Warm-Up: Mini-Russian Circle

8 MINUTES

- Player 1 leaves the corner and receives a pass from the opposite corner; he then goes in and shoots.
- Immediately after, the player who passed to the first player leaves the corner and receives a puck from the opposite corner.
- He shoots on the net.

Focus

- Making accurate passes
- Presenting a good target for a pass
- Taking a quality shot hitting the net

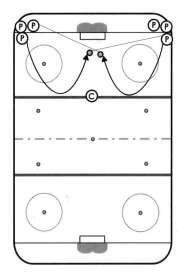

Passing Warm-Up:
Mini-Russian Circle

One-on-One: Touchdown
8 MINUTES

- Coach chips a puck into the corner. (You can run this drill out of both corners.)
- Two players compete for the puck. (Tell players to stay on their respective side of the ice.)
- The defensive player competes for the puck while trying to keep his body between the player with the puck and the two cones.
- The offensive player tries to skate the puck between the two cones.

Focus
- Not overcommitting to the puck
- Controlling the puck under pressure
- Having fun

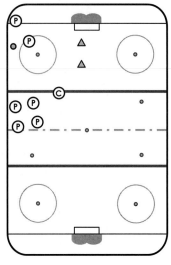

One-on-One: Touchdown

Quinnipiac Plays: Two-on-One: Two-Pass
8 MINUTES

- On the whistle, F1 passes to D.
- D then passes to F2.
- Players go straight two-on-one down the ice.
- Players must stay on their side until they cross the far blue line.

Focus
- Force shot to come from outside forward.
- D gaps up on attacking forwards.
- Forwards attack D with speed.

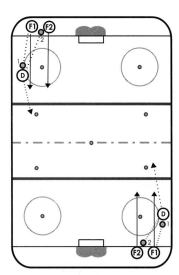

Quinnipiac Plays: Two-on-One: Two-Pass

Two-on-Two: Two Times Touchdown
8 MINUTES

- Coach chips a puck into the corner. (You can run this drill out of both corners.)
- Four players compete for the puck, two on one team, two on the other. (Tell players to stay on their respective side of the ice.)
- The defensive players compete for the puck while trying to keep their bodies between the player with the puck and the two cones.
- The offensive players try to skate the puck between the two cones.
- If there is a change in control, the players must make at least one pass to skate through the cones for a touchdown.

Focus
- Not overcommitting to the puck
- Controlling the puck under pressure
- Having fun

Two-on-Two: Two Times Touchdown

Three-on-Two: Point Shot to Straight Three-on-Two, Phase One and Phase Two

8 MINUTES (for both phases)

- X1 starts the drill by passing a puck to D1.
- D1 passes the puck to D2, who shoots on the net.
- All three Xs crash the net for the rebound.
- After the rebound is played, Coach chips a puck to one of the three Xs, who heads up the ice attacking the defensive players, three-on-two.

Focus

- Forwards gain control of the far blue line.
- Both defensemen stay between the dots on the rush.
- The Xs make a play on the net by the top of the circles.

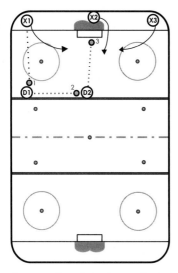

Three-on-Two: Point Shot to Straight Three-on-Two, Phase One

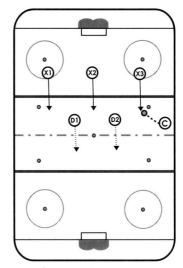

Three-on-Two: Point Shot to Straight Three-on-Two, Phase Two

Small Games: Three-on-Three with Coach as Change of Possession

10 MINUTES

- Coach dumps in a puck.
- The first team to gain possession and get the puck back to Coach is on offense.
- The other team plays defense. If they gain possession, they need to get the puck to Coach to go on offense.
- Emphasize moving to get open and covering the open player.

Focus

- Transition from offense to defense

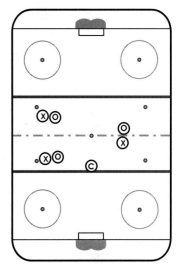

Small Games: Three-on-Three with Coach as Change of Possession

Practice Drills, Ages 9–10

The following drills are appropriate for players ages 9–10.

Skating Warm-Up: Circles, Phase One and Phase Two

5 MINUTES (for both phases)

Three players skate around the outside of the circles. Players cross feet over as they go around. Players go around each circle one and one-half times before proceeding to the next circle.

- First time, players skate forward.
- Second time, players skate backward.
- Third time, players face one direction the whole time and must pivot forward and backward at the top and bottom of each circle.

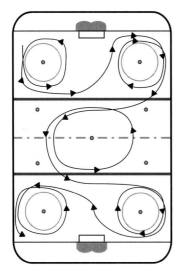

Skating Warm-Up: Circles,
Phase One

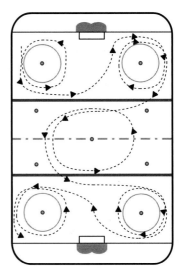

Circles, Phase Two

Focus

- Quality crossovers (big initial push and cross under)
- Keeping feet moving at all times
- Staying low to the ice and maintaining speed while carrying a puck

Passing Warm-Up: Inside-Out Russian Circle

5 MINUTES

- This is similar to the Mini-Russian Circle; however, players go inside-out around the cones.
- Player 1 starts without the puck and receives a pass from the opposite corner. She takes a shot and sets up in front of the net.
- Player 2 goes after making the pass and receives a puck from the opposite corner. She takes a shot and sets up in front of the net.
- Coach then shoots a puck at the net, with both players competing for the rebound.
- Coach blows the whistle, and a new set of players start.

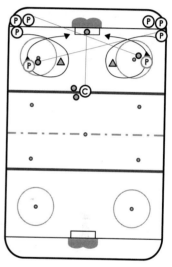

Passing Warm-Up: Inside-Out Russian Circle

Quinnipiac Plays: Shooting One-on-None

5 MINUTES

This drill involves windmill shooting.

- The players line up in opposite corners.
- Player 1 leaves without a puck and cuts the far blue line.
- Player 1 receives a pass from the second player in line.
- Player 2 then repeats what Player 1 did.
- The drill is continuous.

Focus
- Hit net on shot
- Lead player with pass

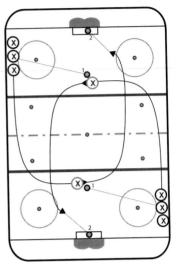

Quinnipiac Plays: Shooting One-on-None

Two-on-None: Swing

5 MINUTES

This drill is run out of both ends simultaneously. Once the drill starts, it is continuous and no whistle is needed.

- Both X1 and X2 leave at the same time without pucks. Once they hit the tops of the circles at the far end, X2 receives a pass from X5.
- X2 then moves the puck up to X1.
- X1 crosses over the blue line and delays with a tight turn.

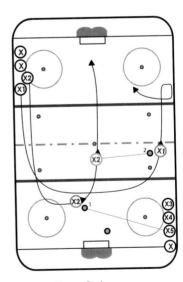

Two-on-None: Swing

- X2 continues to drive the net.
- X1 has two options:
  1. Hit X2 backdoor.
  2. Take a shot and have X2 drive the net for a rebound.

Focus
- Allowing the second player to join the rush by delaying
- A quick play on the net from the top of the circle

One-on-One: Little Boss
8 MINUTES

- Player 1 skates around the far cone and picks up the puck.
- Player 2 skates to the closer cone and pivots to face the oncoming player by backpedaling.
- They play one-on-one to the net.
- All players play both the defensive and offensive positions.

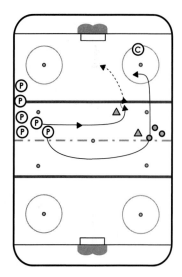

One-on-One: Little Boss

Two-on-One: Breakout Overlap
8 MINUTES

- The defender lines up in the corner with pucks.
- The forwards line up at the blue lines.
- On the whistle, the defender circles the net and makes a breakout pass to the forwards, who have skated down and posted up on the wall.
- The forwards skate out of the zone and overlap.
- The defender gaps up, and they play it two-on-one to the net.

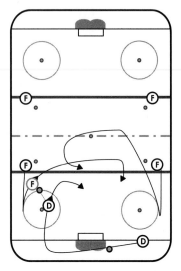

Two-on-One: Breakout Overlap

Focus
- Forwards get a shot on net.
- The defender gaps up on the two forwards.

Two-on-Two: Big Loop
8 MINUTES

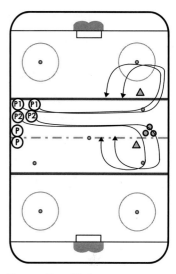

- On the whistle, both Player 1s skate around the defensive cone and take a defensive posture.
- Player 2s skate around the offensive cone and pick up a puck; they then attack the defensive players two-on-two.

Focus
- Introduce concept of man-to-man coverage two-on-two.
- Introduce the idea of angling to defensive players.

Two-on-Two: Big Loop

- Be creative, remain on side, and get a shot (for offensive players).
- Make it competitive: ask players to count how many shots and goals they get.
- Keep track of the number of shots (for defensive players).

Three-on-Two: Regroup to Three-on-None to Three-on-Two, Phase One

8 MINUTES (for both phases)

- Coach starts the drill by chipping a puck to the far blue line.
- Both defenders go back to get it.
- The defenders make one pass to each other before they pass it to one of the forwards.
- All three forwards come back to support the defenders, maintaining eye contact with the puck at all times.
- The forwards then attack, three-on-none.

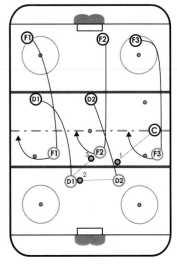

Three-on-Two: Regroup to Three-on-None to Three-on-Two, Phase One

Three-on-Two: Regroup to Three-on-None to Three-on-Two, Phase Two

- Coach chips another puck, this time to the forwards, who attack the defenders, three-on-two.
- Have forwards attack the net in the form of a triangle.

Focus
- Quick puck movement
- Forwards have passing options in all three lanes (both outside lanes and the middle lane).
- Defenders try to force the shot from the outside on three-on-two.
- Forwards use offensive triangle to attack the net.

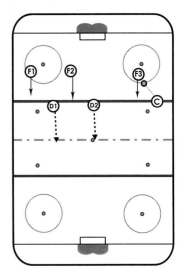

Three-on-Two: Regroup to Three-on-None to Three-on-Two, Phase Two

Small Games: Treasure Island
8 MINUTES

- Set up two nets back-to-back on each hash mark.
- Players need to gain possession of the puck and pass it to the coach who is designated for their team.
- The coach passes the puck back, and they attack the net that their coach is facing.
- Defensive team wants to gain possession and get the puck to the other side.

Focus
- Transitioning from offense to defense

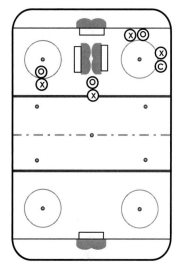

Small Games: Treasure Island

Practice Drills, Ages 11–12

The following drills are appropriate for players ages 11–12.

Skating Warm-Up: Bobcat Two Circle, Phase One and Phase Two
5 MINUTES (for both phases)

- Three players skate forward, crossing feet over around circle one and one-half times, carrying a puck.
- Players then proceed to circle the neutral zone, skating through all offside dots.
- Once they hit the far blue line, they coast to the corner.
- First time, players skate forward.
- Second time, players skate backward.
- Third time, players face one direction the whole time (players must pivot forward and backward at each circle and between offside dots).

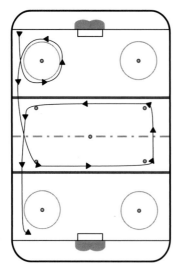

Skating Warm-Up: Bobcat Two Circle, Phase One

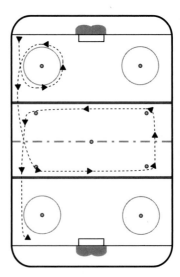

Bobcat Two Circle, Phase Two

Focus

- Quality crossovers (big initial push and cross under)
- Keeping feet moving at all times and maintaining speed when changing direction
- Staying low to the ice during pivots

Passing Warm-Up: Cheechoo Two-Touch
5 MINUTES

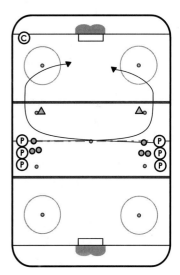

- Player 1 starts with the puck and skates along the red line.
- As he skates along the red line, he passes to the first player on the opposite line.
- These players exchange passes two more times. As soon as the final pass is delivered, the first player in the opposite line leaves with a puck.
- He executes the same passes with the opposite line.

Passing Warm-Up: Cheechoo Two-Touch

Focus

- Skating with speed and making crisp exchanges as quickly as possible while remaining under control
- Quick passes that are under control
- Communication between players for the puck

Shooting Drill: Three-Shooter

5 MINUTES

- Set up lines in opposite corners.
- First three players in each line will go.
- X1 makes a straight sprint to the top of the circle and takes a shot.
- X2 skates past the red line and cuts to the middle of the ice, and then heads to the net for a shot.
- X3 skates past the red line, cuts to the far side and around the outside dot, and then cuts to the net for a shot.

Focus

- Shoot in stride

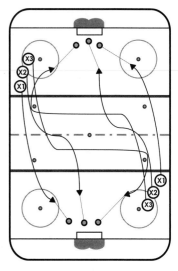

Shooting Drill: Three-Shooter

Two-on-None: Double Two-on-None, Phase One

5 MINUTES (for both phases)

- X1 starts the drill by making a pass to X2.
- From X1's pass, both X1 and X2 will skate out to the neutral zone, overlap, and exchange the puck.
- Both Xs, while staying onside, attack the net two-on-none.

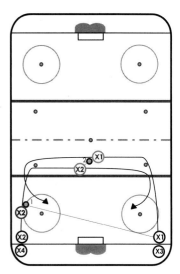

Two-on-None: Double Two-on-None, Phase One

Two-on-None: Double Two-on-None, Phase Two

- After the initial rush, X1 and X2 curl and receive a puck from X3.
- X1 and X2 then skate the full length of the ice and attack the far net.
- As a variation, X3 can also join X1 and X2 after making the pass to make it a three-on-none.

Focus

- On the overlap, making sure the puck-carrier always stays between the net and the player he is exchanging the puck with
- Making sure that on the rush a play is made by the top of the circles, either a shot or a backdoor pass
- Keeping all passes in front of the player
- Attacking with speed

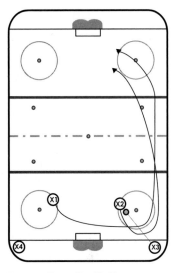

Two-on-None: Double Two-on-None, Phase Two

One-on-One: Chameleon
8 MINUTES

- Player 1 skates around the far cone and picks up the puck.
- Player 2 skates to the closer cone and pivots to face the oncoming player by backpedaling.
- They play one-on-one to the net.
- All players play both the defensive and offensive positions:
  1. After the initial one-on-one is over, the two players will change roles.
  2. The defensive player will transition to the offense and look to get into position to receive a pass from Coach.
  3. The offensive player will transition to defense and look to defend against the pass and the offensive player.

One-on-One: Chameleon

Focus
- Positioning
- Communicating for the puck

Quinnipiac Plays: Two-on-One: Overspeed
8 MINUTES

- Forwards line up on either hash mark, defenders at the blue line.
- On the whistle, forwards skate high and low around the two circles.
- Defender skates forward to the point in between the circles, creating good gap, and then pivots backward to play two-on-one.
- Forwards stay wide and head up the ice, two-on-one.

Focus
- Defensemen work on gap control.
- Forwards use quick feet and attack with speed.

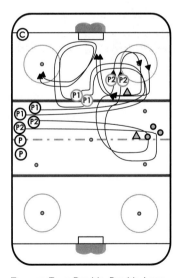

Quinnipiac Plays: Two-on-One: Overspeed

Two-on-Two: Double-Double Loop
8 MINUTES

- On the whistle, both Player 1s skate around the defensive cone and take a defensive posture.
- Both Players 2s skate around the offensive cone and pick up a puck; they then attack P1 defensive players, two-on-two.
- After players attack and the play is completed, Coach will blow the whistle.
- All four players must jump up and touch the blue line. The offensive players become defensive, the defensive players become offensive.

Two-on-Two: Double-Double Loop

- Coach can make a direct pass to an attacking player or chip into an area of the ice to promote a battle.
- Play continues until a goal or a shot or until Coach blows the whistle.

Focus
- Gap control
- Transition

Three-on-Two: Overspeed
8 MINUTES

- On the whistle, F1 carries the puck and leaves for F3.
- Both defenders (D1 and D2) skate to the top of the circles and pivot backward to accept the rush.
- Forwards must stay on the outside of the circle at all times.

Focus
- Forwards keep feet moving and work on skating (edges and balance).
- Defenders work on gapping up on the forwards.

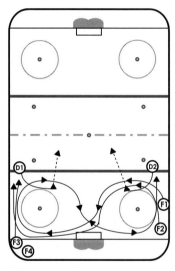

Three-on-Two: Overspeed

Small Games: Gretzky Game
8 MINUTES

- Set up two nets equal with the dots on the goal line.
- One player from each team must stay below the goal line.
- The two players from each team above the goal line must stay above.
- Players above the goal line must get the puck to the player below before they can score.
- Players can score on any net.

Focus
- Getting shots with traffic
- Competitive drill

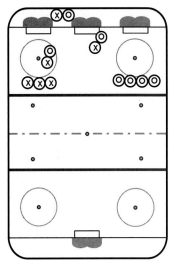

Small Games: Gretzky Game

Practice Drills, Ages 13–14

The following drills are appropriate for players ages 13–14.

Skating Warm-Up: Canuck Warm-Up
5 MINUTES

- Player skates forward to the bottom of the circle and pivots backward to hash marks.
- At hash marks, the player pivots forward to the bottom of the far circle.
- At the bottom of the far circle, the player turns and skates backward to the blue line.
- Once the player reaches the blue line, she stops and sidesteps back to the original starting point.
- Split team in half and use both ends of the rink. Start the next player when the first player reaches the bottom of the first circle.

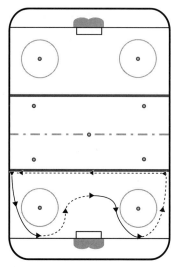

Skating Warm-Up: Canuck Warm-Up

Focus
- Keeping body low while pivoting
- Maintaining speed while pivoting
- When sidestepping, keeping feet and shoulders square to end boards at all times (lateral movement)

Passing Warm-Up: Moose Factory Three-Strike

5 MINUTES

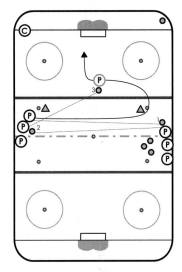

- Player 1 starts with the puck, skating along the red line.
- He passes to the first player in line on the opposite line.
- The player receives the puck and makes a pass to the first player in line in the opposite line.
- The original player times his skating route to receive a pass from the player in the line from where he started and looks to receive the puck in the middle of the ice.
- The next player in the opposite line from where the last pass was made is the next player to go.

Passing Warm-Up: Moose Factory Three-Strike

Focus
- Good passes
- Learning to accept passes on forehand and backhand

Quinnipiac Plays: Shooting One-on-None: High-Low Shooting

5 MINUTES

- Set up lines in all four corners.
- X1 skates up the ice, swings around the near neutral zone face-off dots, and cuts in for a shot on the opposite side from the start.
- X2 skates around the second neutral zone face-off dots and skates in for a shot from the opposite side from the start.
- Both sides play at the same time.

Focus

- Shooting in stride

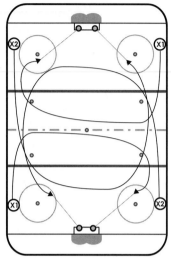

Quinnipiac Plays: Shooting One-on-None: High-Low Shooting

Two-on-None: Four Blue Double Regroup

5 MINUTES

- X1 (with puck) and X2 start the drill by creating an overlap, exchanging, and then both turning up the ice.
- X2 then makes a pass to O1, who passes to O2.
- X1 and X2 then regroup with Os.
- O2 moves the puck up to either X1 or X2.
- X1 and X2 attack the net two-on-none.
- After Os make passes to Xs, they start the drill from the other side.

In a variation, create a three-on-none by activating O2 after she makes the pass.

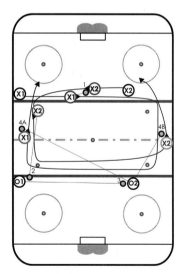

Two-on-None: Four Blue Double Regroup

Focus

- Firm passes
- Head player or lead player with pass
- Attacking the net with speed

One-on-One: Dog Versus Bug

8 MINUTES

- On the whistle, F1 skates around the far cone with a puck and then attacks the net.
- F2 skates around the closer cone and angles to defend one-on-one against the attacking forward (all players are skating forward).
- After the shot or play is defended, the forward looks to receive a pass from Coach, who should pass only once the player has positioned himself to receive the pass.

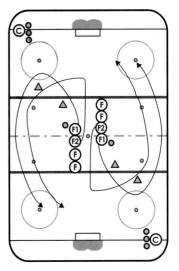

One-on-One: Dog Versus Bug

Focus

- Positioning
- Defending the play

Another Option

- Place pucks in a corner.
- Players follow the same path, but the attacking player does not have a puck. The defensive player must skate forward.
- He attacks the net solely looking for a position to receive a puck from Coach. Defensive player looks to maintain position.
- After the pass from Coach, the offensive player picks up the puck and circles back to attack the net against the defensive player.

All-Purpose Two-on-One, Phase One

8 MINUTES (for both phases)

- One side plays at a time.
- Forwards are in all four corners, defenders at the blue line.
- On the whistle, F1 passes to D1, D1 then shoots.
- After the shot, F1 makes cross-ice pass to F2.
- F1 and F2 attempt a goal at the other end, with D1 defending.

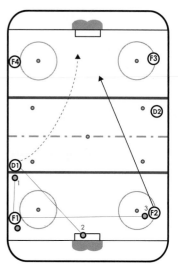

All-Purpose Two-on-One,
Phase One

All-Purpose Two-on-One, Phase Two

- Start once F1, F2, and D1 have completed their full-ice two-on-one.
- On the whistle, F3 passes to D2.
- F1, F2, and D1 battle two-on-one in front of the net.
- D2 shoots.
- The drill continues in the opposite direction.

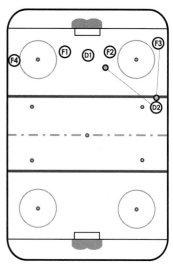

All-Purpose Two-on-One,
Phase Two

Two-on-Two: Double-Double Loop and Attack, Phase One

8 MINUTES (for all three phases)

- On the whistle, both Player 1s skate around the defensive cone and take a defensive posture.
- Player 2s skate around the offensive cone and pick up a puck; they then attack the two defensive players two-on-two.
- After players attack and the play is completed, Coach blows the whistle.

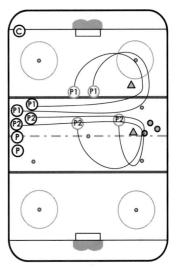

Two-on-Two: Double-Double Loop and Attack, Phase One

Two-on-Two: Double-Double Loop and Attack, Phase Two

- All four players must jump up and touch the blue line. The offensive players become defensive, the defensive players become offensive.
- Coach can make a direct pass to an attacking player or chip into an area of the ice to promote a battle.
- Play continues until a goal or a shot or until Coach blows the whistle.

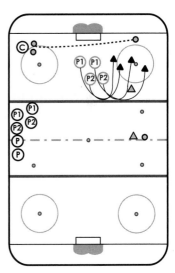

Two-on-Two: Double-Double Loop and Attack, Phase Two

Two-on-Two: Double-Double Loop and Attack, Phase Three

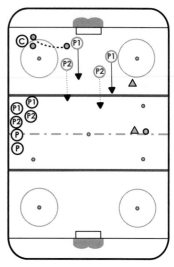

- Once Coach blows the whistle, the last offensive group receives a pass from the coach and attacks the length of the ice.
- They will be attacking the last defensive group from the pairings at the other end of the rink.
- The last defensive group must immediately move to close the gap between them and the attacking players.

Two-on-Two: Double-Double Loop and Attack, Phase Three

Focus

- Remember that the three phases are: attack two-on-two, defense and offense switch and attack the same net, and attack the length of the ice. This is a great conditioning drill that simulates the many changes from offense to defense.

Breakout to Three-on-None to Three-on-Two, Phase One

8 MINUTES (for both phases)

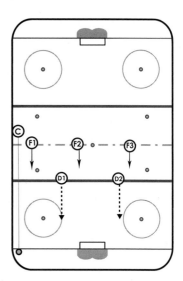

- Coach starts the drill by dumping the puck in the zone.
- Both the defenders and the three forwards go back and break the puck out of the zone.
- The three forwards attack three-on-none.

Breakout to Three-on-None to Three-on-Two, Phase One

Breakout to Three-on-None to Three-on-Two, Phase Two

- Coach chips a puck to the three forwards, who attack the two defenders who have followed up the play.
- A three-on-two is played all the way back to the net.

Focus

- The team focuses on breakouts.
- Forwards focus on attacking with an offensive triangle.
- Defenders follow play closely so they always maintain good gap.

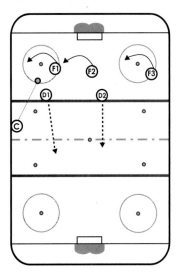

Breakout to Three-on-None to Three-on-Two, Phase Two

Small Games: Tip, Screen, Rebound

8 MINUTES

- Teams will be trying to score on the net they are facing.
- Players in the zone must work to get possession and then pass to their defender or point player.
- They then must go to the net for a tip screen or one crack at a rebound. Defender must shoot.
- Team without the puck must defend and try to get the puck to their side.

Focus

- Goalies playing with traffic in front

Small Games: Tip, Screen, Rebound

Practice Drills, High School and Junior Hockey

The following drills are appropriate for players on high school and junior league teams.

Skating Warm-Up: Tiger Warm-Up, Phase One and Phase Two

5 MINUTES (for both phases)

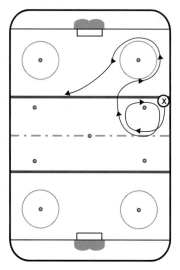

Skating Warm-Up: Tiger Warm-Up, Phase One

- Player starts on the blue line and begins skating to the red line, at which point he begins crossing feet over toward the middle of the ice.
- Player turns back to the blue line once he hits the middle dot.
- Player continues to cross feet over as he heads back to the red line.
- Once hitting the red line for the second time, player heads down around the near circle.
- The drill finishes as the player accelerates through the blue line.
- For Phase Two, repeat Phase One, with the player skating backward the entire time.

Focus

- Staying low and never stop moving feet during crossovers
- Staying well balanced while in a small area
- Working both inside and outside edges of skates
- Staying inside the red and blue lines

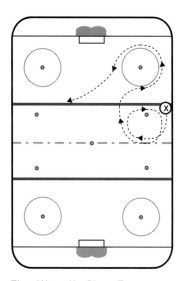

Tiger Warm-Up, Phase Two

Passing Warm-Up: Squamish Wheel, Phase One and Phase Two

5 MINUTES (for both phases)

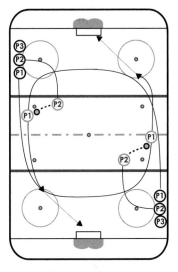

- The first players in each line start without pucks. (You can run this drill on both sides of the ice.)
- They skate down at full speed to the tops of the circles, and then cut and move directly up the far boards.
- The second players in each line move their feet and step out away from the boards to the middle of the ice.
- P2 hits P1 with a direct pass.
- P2 from each line follows the same route as P1.
- P3 then steps out and makes the pass to P2.
- The drill is continuous.

Passing Warm-Up: Squamish Wheel, Phase One

Focus

- Shoot in stride
- Tape-to-tape passes

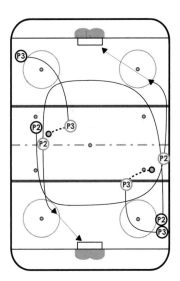

Passing Warm-Up: Squamish Wheel, Phase Two

Quinnipiac Plays: Shooting One-on-Goalie

5 MINUTES

- This drill has a triple swing.
- To start the drill, X1 has the puck in front of the net.
- On the whistle, X1 shoots and then swings to the corner, picking up a puck.
- X2 swings to the top of the circle and receives a pass from X1.
- X3 swings to the blue line and receives a pass from X2.
- X3 goes in for a shot, and then picks up a puck and starts the other side.

Focus

- Good timing

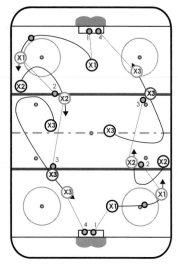

Quinnipiac Plays: Shooting
One-on-Goalie

Two-on-None: Bobcat Series

5 MINUTES

- X2 starts the drill by making a rink-wide pass to X1.
- X2 and X1 continue to make passes up the ice.
- Whichever X has the puck once they reach the red line passes it to either O.
- The Os exchange the puck between themselves before making a pass back to the Xs, who are streaking up the ice on a two-on-none.
- The Os continue the drill once they have moved the puck to the Xs.

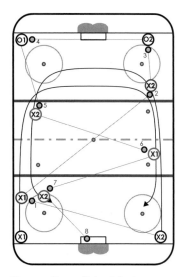

Two-on-None: Bobcat Series

In a variation, the last O to touch the puck can join the rush to make it a three-on-none.

Focus
- Making backhand passes
- Receiving backhand passes

One-on-One: New Haven
8 MINUTES

- F1 passes the puck to defender at the point.
- Defender carries the puck to the middle of the ice and takes a shot from the point.
- After the initial pass, F1 goes to the net for a deflection rebound opportunity.
- F1 in front of the net skates on angle back to the wall and receives a pass from F2 in line.
- F1 then drives the length of the ice one-on-one.
- After the initial one-on-one, F1 tries to reposition to receive a pass from Coach in the corner.
- Defensive player looks to position himself to defend.

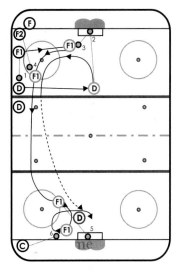

One-on-One: New Haven

Quinnipiac Plays: Hoppy Neutral Zone Two-on-One

8 MINUTES

- Forwards and pucks are at center ice; defenders are at opposite blue lines. (You can run this drill on both ends of the rink.)
- F1 passes to D and then skates inside the blue line and loops to the far side.
- F2 delays to support F1.
- D receives possession and backpedals, and then steps toward F1 and makes a cross-ice pass.
- Defenders must then gap up as the two forwards from the other side will be coming for a two-on-one.

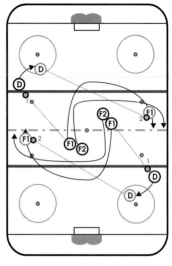

Quinnipiac Plays: Hoppy Neutral Zone Two-on-One

Focus
- Gap control

Two-on-Two: Cornell Continuous Transition

8 MINUTES

- On the whistle, a one-on-one starts between F1 and D1, which extends the length of the ice.
- As the one-on-one comes to a conclusion, Coach blows the whistle again. This starts a one-on-one between F2 and D2.
- The same whistle also indicates to F1 and D1 to end their one-on-one and jump into the play with F2 and D2—D1 joins the rush as the offensive player and F2 joins the rush as the defensive player.

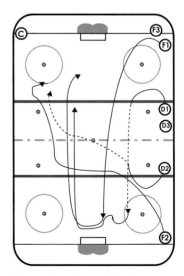

Two-on-Two: Cornell Continuous Transition

- F2 must judge his attack to take into account the offensive player joining the rush as well as the defensive check coming back.
- On the next whistle, F1 and D1 are no longer in the play and F2 and D2 switch roles to join the attack started by F3 and D3.
- The drill is continuous.

Focus
- Communicating
- Keeping head up as the puck-carrier to read the play
- Ensuring athletes respect offside rules

Three-on-Two: Three-on-None Build, Phase One
8 MINUTES (for both phases)

- Three forwards leave with a puck, and each takes a quick wrist shot.
- F1 takes a puck from the corner and the three forwards attack D1, three-on-one.

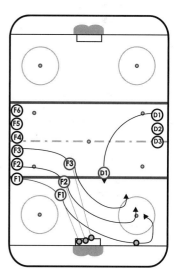

Three-on-Two: Three-on-None Build, Phase One

Three-on-Two: Three-on-None Build, Phase Two

- After the play on the net, D1 outlets the three same forwards from Phase One, who attack D2 and D3 three-on-two.
- F6 starts the drill going the other way after the first unit has crossed the red line.

Focus

- Forwards attack the offensive blue line with speed.
- Defenders try to keep shots from the rush to the outside.
- Both defenders and forwards make decisions in transition.

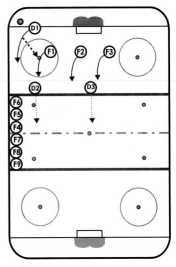

Three-on-Two: Three-on-None Build, Phase Two

Small Games: Outnumber Game

8 MINUTES

- Drill begins one-on-one.
- Coach dumps a puck, and players battle.
- A player can be added by either team by passing to their line.
- Teams can have up to four players in the game.
- Players must pass to Coach to go on offense.

Focus

- Puck movement
- Competition

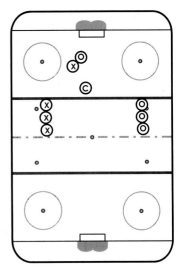

Small Games: Outnumber Game

Practice Drills, College

The following drills are appropriate for players on college teams.

Combo, Phase One

5 MINUTES (for both phases)

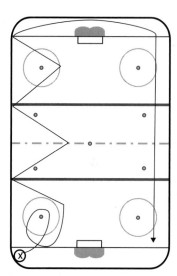

- Player makes a tight power turn around the dot and comes back to the circle. He then crosses over around the circle and accelerates to the blue line.
- Once player reaches the blue line, he uses his inside leg to stop on the inside edge and pivot, changing direction on one foot, before skating to the red line, where he repeats the inside foot stop and pivot.
- The player repeats this zigzag pattern down the ice as shown in the diagram.

Combo, Phase One

- Upon finishing the zigzag pattern, the player skates around the net and begins skating forward up the ice.
- When player is skating up the ice, he strides with one leg and then recovers before pushing with the other leg (there should be a two-second glide before the other leg pushes).

Focus

- Using the inside of the skate
- Balancing while changing direction
- Using long strides (full extension)
- Recovering the leg (after each leg push, the foot must come back underneath the body)

Combo, Phase Two

- Repeat the same pattern as Phase One; however, player stops by using his outside foot (using the outside edge to pivot and change direction).
- Player skates backward behind the goal and up the ice, working on C cuts.

Focus
- The C cut while still maintaining the glide
- Returning the push leg underneath her body for full recovery

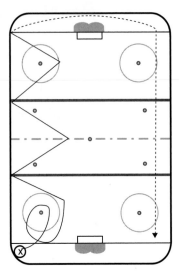

Combo, Phase Two

Passing Warm-Up: Squamish Advanced
5 MINUTES

- P1s in each line start without pucks.
- They skate down at full speed to the tops of the circles, and then cut and move directly up the far boards.
- P2s in each line are moving their feet and step out away from the boards to the middle of the ice.
- P2s hit P1s with an indirect pass off the boards.
- P2s from each line then follow the same route as P1s.
- P3s step out and make the pass to P2s.

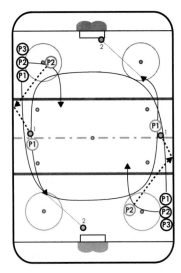

Passing Warm-Up: Squamish Advanced

Advanced Options

- First passes made must be indirect off the boards.
- Two passes must be exchanged between the two players.
- Players must shoot well before the tops of the circles and then receive a pass from Coach for a second shot.

Focus

- Firm passes
- Quick play on the net

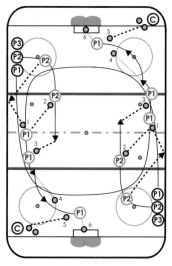

Squamish Advanced,
Advanced Options

One-on-None: Give and Go Long Pass

5 MINUTES

- On the whistle, X1 passes to X2, and then skates straight down the ice. (You can play both sides of the rink, although only one side is shown in the diagram.)
- X2 passes the puck back to X1, who goes in for a shot and swings to pick up another puck.
- After passing to X1, X2 makes one full rotation around the center ice, and then cuts to the boards to receive a pass from X1, while staying on the side.
- X2 goes in for a shot.

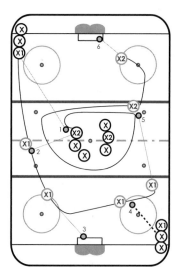

One-on-None: Give and Go Long
Pass

Two-on-None: Boston Rebound

5 MINUTES

- X1 shoots, and X2 crashes in for a rebound.
- X1 outlets X3, who hits X2.
- The drill is continuous.

Focus

- Driving the net for rebounds
- Moving the puck up the ice quickly

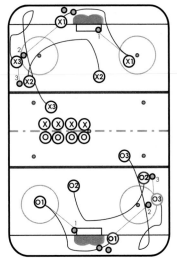

Two-on-None: Boston Rebound

One-on-One: Surrey Eagle Gap

8 MINUTES

- Forward drives directly at the defender with the puck. (You can play this drill on both sides of the rink.)
- The defender acquires the forward and plays him one-on-one.
- If Coach blows the whistle, the forward must immediately change direction and attack the other net.
- The defender must immediately reacquire the new forward by attacking the play and then backpedaling to control the gap.
- If Coach does not blow the whistle, the defender must maintain a strong gap on the initial one-on-one.
- Coach should blow the whistle only after the opposite forward is on the end farthest from the opposite defender.

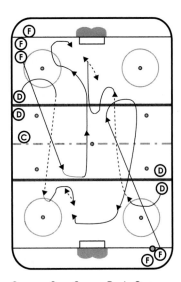

One-on-One: Surrey Eagle Gap

Focus

- Keeping head up in the neutral zone (forward)
- Being quick to close gap while remaining under control (defender)

Two-Hitter Two-on-One

8 MINUTES

- Defenders are in opposite corners with pucks; forwards are at all four blue lines.
- On the whistle, D1 passes to D2, who shoots.
- D1 then passes to F1, who skates toward D1 and bumps the puck back to D2.
- F1 and F2 overlap, and D2 gives them a pass. They then go two-on-one on D2.
- D1 trails the play and then gets a pass from D3.
- D1 shoots, and the drill begins the other way.

Two-Hitter Two-on-One

Focus

- Gap.
- Activate defense in offensive rush.

Two-on-Two: Tsawwassen Tangle

8 MINUTES

- Offensive P1s are a team playing two-on-two against defensive P2s.
- On the whistle, P1s and P2s engage in battle against each other in the one zone.
- After a goal, a clearing play, or the whistle, the defensive P2s break out of the zone looking for a pass.
- Coach hits P2s with a pass as they attack defensive P3s waiting in the neutral zone.
- P2s attack P3s in the opposing end zone. P3s cannot make a defensive move on P2s until after they have crossed the red line.
- P4s must be ready to hop into the neutral zone as the next defensive pair.
- After the attack, a clearing play, a goal, or the whistle, P3s break out of the zone.
- They will receive a pass from Coach as they attack P4s.
- Drill is continuous.

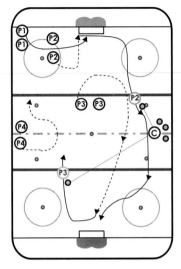

Two-on-Two: Tsawwassen Tangle

Focus
- Competitive
- Defense work on gap

Bobcat Build, Phase One: Breakout to Three-on-Two

8 MINUTES (for all four phases)

- Coach dumps one puck in. There must be a defender-to-defender pass, and then a quick pass up to a forward.
- All three forwards must touch the puck.
- The last forward to touch the puck goes in for a shot.

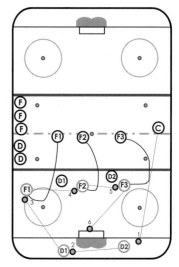

Bobcat Build, Phase One:
Breakout to Three-on-Two

Bobcat Build, Phase Two: Two-on-Two

- F1 and F2 get a pass from Coach.
- F1 and F2 curl back two-on-two against D1 and D2.

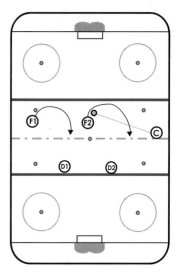

Bobcat Build, Phase Two:
Two-on-Two

Bobcat Build, Phase Three: Two-on-One

- After the two-on-two, F1 and F2 curl back and receive a pass from Coach.
- They play two-on-one against F3, who has gapped up.

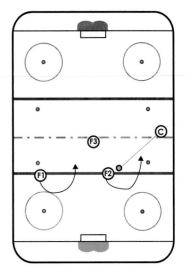

Bobcat Build, Phase Three: Two-on-One

Bobcat Build, Phase Four: Three-on-Two

- Upon the finish of the two-on-one, Coach sends another puck to one of the forwards.
- The forwards attack three-on-two against the defenders.

Focus
- Attacking with speed
- Forcing players to transition quickly

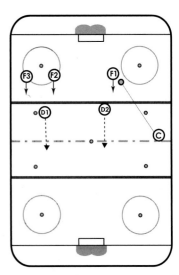

Bobcat Build, Phase Four: Three-on-Two

Small Games: Center Ice Three-on-Four

8 MINUTES

- Game is played in the neutral zone.
- Whichever team has the puck has four players in the neutral zone; the other team has three.
- Once the team without the puck gains it, they will have four players in, while the other team will have one player leave the zone.

Focus
- Puck movement

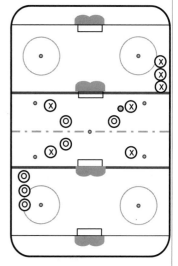

Small Games: Center Ice
Three-on-Four

Index